Yale Language Series

Biblical Hebrew

SUPPLEMENT

FOR

ENHANCED

COMPREHENSION

VICTORIA HOFFER

YALE UNIVERSITY

YALE UNIVERSITY PRESS / NEW HAVEN AND LONDON

Publisher: Mary Jane Peluso

Production Controller: Aldo Cupo

Editorial Assistant: Gretchen Rings

Designed by Mary Valencia.

Set in Meridien type by Integrated Publishing Solutions, Grand Rapids, Michigan.

Printed in the United States of America.

Library of Congress Cataloging-in-Publication Data

Hoffer, Victoria, 1943–

   Biblical Hebrew : supplement for enhanced comprehension.

     p.   cm. — (Yale language series)

   English and Hebrew.

   Includes index.

   ISBN 978-0-300-09863-1 (pbk. : alk. paper)

     1. Hebrew language—Grammar—Textbooks.   2. Hebrew language—Grammar—Problems, exercises, etc.   3. Hebrew language—Grammar—Miscellanea.   I. Kittel, Bonnie Pedrotti. Biblical Hebrew. II. Title. III. Series.

   PJ4567.3.K5 2004 Suppl.

   492.4'82421—dc22   2004044308

A catalogue record for this book is available from the British Library.

The paper in this book meets the guidelines for permanence and durability of the Committee on Production Guidelines for Book Longevity of the Council on Library Resources.

10 9 8 7 6 5 4

CONTENTS

———

CONTENTS

LESSON 6

וַיָּבֹאוּ עַד־הַיַּרְדֵּן הוּא וְכָל־בְּנֵי יִשְׂרָאֵל

LESSON 7

וַיִּתֵּן אַבְרָהָם אֶת־כָּל־אֲשֶׁר־לוֹ לְיִצְחָק

LESSON 8

וְיָדְעוּ כִּי־שְׁמִי יהוה

LESSON 9

וְהֵם לֹא יָדְעוּ כִּי שֹׁמֵעַ יוֹסֵף

CONTENTS

LESSON 10

וַיָּבֹא אֶל־אָבִיו וַיֹּאמֶר אָבִי וַיֹּאמֶר הִנֶּנִּי

31

LESSON 11

וַיֵּצְאוּ לָלֶכֶת אַרְצָה כְּנַעַן וַיָּבֹאוּ אַרְצָה כְּנָעַן

34

LESSON 12

וַיַּרְא כָּל־הָעָם וַיִּפְּלוּ עַל־פְּנֵיהֶם

35

LESSON 13

וַיֹּאמֶר הִנְנִי כִּי קָרָאתָ לִי

37

LESSON 14

כִּי־תִשְׁמֹר אֶת־כָּל־הַמִּצְוָה הַזֹּאת לַעֲשֹׂתָהּ

39

CONTENTS

LESSON 18

שְׁמַע יִשְׂרָאֵל יהוה אֱלֹהֵינוּ יהוה אֶחָד: 54

LESSON 19

וְאָמַרְתָּ דִּבֶּר יהוה כִּי שֹׁמֵעַ עַבְדֶּךָ   56

LESSON 20

וַיִּקְרָא פַרְעֹה אֶל־מֹשֶׁה וַיֹּאמֶר לְכוּ עִבְדוּ אֶת־יהוה   57

LESSON 21

וַיִּקַּח יִשְׂרָאֵל אֵת כָּל־הֶעָרִים הָאֵלֶּה וַיֵּשֶׁב יִשְׂרָאֵל בְּכָל־עָרֵי הָאֱמֹרִי   58

CONTENTS

CONTENTS

➤

LESSON 27

וְלֹא־שָׁבוּ אֶל־יהוה אֱלֹהֵיהֶם   67

LESSON 28

וְהַמֶּלֶךְ אָסָא הִשְׁמִיעַ אֶת־כָּל־יְהוּדָה   70

LESSON 29

וְהָיָה אֱלֹהִים עִמָּכֶם וְהֵשִׁיב אֶתְכֶם אֶל־אֶרֶץ אֲבֹתֵיכֶם   73

LESSON 30

הַגִּידָה לִי מֶה עָשִׂיתָה   76

CONTENTS

LESSON 39

LESSON 40

LESSON 41

LESSON 42

LESSON 43

CONTENTS

LESSON 44

LESSON 45

LESSON 46

LESSON 47

LESSON 48

LESSON 49

CONTENTS

—

INTRODUCTION

As stated briefly in the introduction to the textbook, the purpose of the Supplement is twofold: to provide reinforcement and review, and to go into further detail on some topics that are only touched on in the lessons.

One may ask, Why the review? Are there not exercises aplenty after each lesson? Years of teaching have convinced me that most students require multiple repetitions and variety in presentation in order to absorb and securely retain concepts. The Supplement's question-and-answer format, its sprinkling of true-or-false challenges, and numerous quizlets keep interest high and are meant to be fun. They give students opportunities to test themselves and to get instant feedback. No answer is further than a footnote away. The Supplement is not a simple redundancy, since the questions address topics differently from their explanations in the textbook. What this volume is <u>not</u>, however, is a replacement for studying the lessons. If used as it should be, which is after the student has studied the material in a particular lesson or group of lessons, it should provide a gauge as to how well the concepts have been absorbed.

A subtopic of reinforcement and review is that oh-so-difficult aspect of Biblical Hebrew: vocabulary. There simply cannot be too much review to help inculcate words, especially as they change when in the plural, suffixed, before a maqqef, or in construct. For these reasons, a separate section devoted to vocabulary review has been added at the end. Although the exercises treat words in groups of ten, not every word is in a phrase or sentence in its assigned group; some may appear a lesson or two later to accommodate a particular grammatical construction or concept not presented at the time the word is. If one studies the vocabulary list, does these exercises, reviews the readings, and works with ⊛ הַדְּבָרִים אֵלֶּה one will have a variety of input from which to build up a solid base for word retention.

The other important function of the Supplement is to provide further detail which, if added to the textbook, would make it unwieldy. Some of these more extensive treatments are considered to be useful at the present stage of learning; they are designated **S**. But the references prefaced with S address topics that one or two people in a class almost always seem to ask about but may not be needed "now." The most notorious of these, addressed in S **5**, has to do with vowel changes as nouns change number or state or have suffixes added. Lesson 5 seemed a premature place to discuss such a complex topic, but that is when the questions first seem to come up. Besides, since this is a book, and the item is highlighted, one can always come back to this discussion when one is ready. The short treatments of most of these topics are not meant to be comprehensive. They are meant to provide an introduction until one is ready for the in-depth discussions of the reference grammars.

A word about the organization of the Supplement. A serious attempt was made to cover the topics, large and small, in some sort of systematic manner. It didn't work. Examination of a number of other textbooks confirmed that the organization of Biblical Hebrew texts is somewhat arbitrary. Thus, it seemed to make most sense to mirror the organization of the parent textbook.

One significant way in which the Supplement differs from the textbook is that it uses some examples that are not from the Biblical corpus. This decision, reluctantly made, allowed a more flexible treatment of some topics, especially vocabulary. For this violation of purity we beg lenience.

READING AND WRITING

THE HEBREW ALPHABET

S A Circle the letters below that are final forms:

? פ ע ץ ף ס כ דּ ו צ נ ם מ ס¹

? Letters that look alike tend to confuse. Write the sounds of the following:

___ ם ___ ס ___ מ ___ כ ___ ב ___ פ

___ ז ___ ו ___ ג ___ נ ___ ר ___ ד

___ ה ___ ח ___ ת²

? Dagesh changes the sounds of some letters. Write the sounds of the following:

___ פּ ___ פ ___ בּ ___ ב

___ ך ___ ךּ ___ כ ___ כּ³

---

1 ע ף דּ ו ם

2 m ם s ס m מ ḥ כ v ב p פ
    z ז v ו g ג n נ r ר d ד
                                     h ה ḥ ח t ת

3   p פּ f פ v ב b בּ
                          ḥ ך k ךּ ḥ כ k כּ

3

VOWEL POINTS

—◆—

S B   Circle the vowel(s) that say **oo** as in zoo. Draw a square around the vowel(s) that say **ah** as in father, draw a diamond around the ones that say **eh** as in heck, and underline the vowels that say **ee** as in eek!

?   ֱ ָ ֳ ִ וֹ ֶ ְי ֵי ָ ַ ו **4**

§ B.1   **Is there a clear distinction between long and short vowels?**

Not as clear as one would like. Below is a rough categorization by class:

A   pataḥ ַ and qamats ָ are short, but qamats is longer than pataḥ.

A/I   segol ֶ is short.

I   ḥireq ִ and tsere ֵ may be short or long, and tsere is longer than ḥireq.

I   plene ḥireq ִי and plene tsere ֵי are long. **5**

U   ḥolem וֹ and sureq וּ and their defectiva spellings ḥolem ֹ and qibbuts ֻ are long; qibbuts ֻ can also be short.

U   qamats ḥatuf ָ is short.

Shewa ְ and the composite shewas ֱ ֳ ֲ are all short.

S B–C   Write the following vowels:

?   **I class** _____   **A class** _____   **long U** _____   **defectiva U** _____
A/I _____   **plene long I** _____   **composite shewas** _____   **6**

S B.2   **Is there any other distinction relevant to vowels?**

Yes. It is important to know which vowels are full. <u>All vowels that don't have shewa are full</u>.

?   Circle the full vowels below:

ֱ ָ ֳ ֹ ֵ ְי ֲ ְ ֳ ַ ֱ **7**

---

4 oo ֻ וּ   **ah** ָ ֲ ַ   **eh** ֱ ֶ   **ee** ִי ֵ ַ

5 To know whether a ḥireq ִ or tsere ֵ is short or a defectiva spelling of plene ḥireq ִי or plene tsere ֵי one has to know the history of the word.

6 I class ִ ֵ   **A class** ֲ ַ   **long U** וּ וֹ ֹ ֻ   **defectiva U** ֹ ֻ
A/I ֶ   **plene long I** ִי ֵי   **composite shewas** ֱ ֳ ֲ

7 ֱ ָ ֶ ֹ ַ ְי ֲ ַ ֳ   are full.

4

VOCALIZATION

———

S B–C

? Write each of the following vowel sounds two ways:

hope ____ ____   flute ____ ____   sleigh ____ ____   machine ____ ____ ⁸

? Writing right to left, transliterate the following sentences into Hebrew:

Use **וֹ** for "w" **הֹ** for "th," and **יֹ** for "j"

Adam ate fruit and so did Eve _____

Moses talked to God face to face _____

Joshua fought the battle of Jericho _____

David was king, but he did not build the temple in Jerusalem _____

_____

The Philistines gave Delilah many pieces of silver _____

_____

S C **What constitutes a syllable in Hebrew?**

A syllable is a unit of a word that begins with a consonant and ends with another consonant or with a vowel.

The word **אָמַר** has two syllables. The first is **אָ** It cannot be **אָם** because that would mean that the second syllable would start with the vowel __ and a syllable must begin with a _____ The second syllable is **מַר**

Consonant + shewa __ can close a syllable. **מִצְרַיִם** (which, by the way, means *Egypt*) has three syllables **מִצְ רַ יִם**

? Draw lines between the syllables of the words below:

אֱלֹהִים אֲשֶׁר יָד נָתַן פָּנִים אֲנִי עַיִן אֶרֶץ יָצָא ⁹

———

⁸ hope **וֹ** or **ֹ**   flute **וּ** or **ֻ**   sleigh **יֶ** or **ֵ**   machine **יִ**

or **ִ**

⁹ אֱלֹ|הִים   אֲ|שֶׁר   יָד   נָ|תַן   פָּ|נִים   אֲ|נִי   עַ|יִן

יָ|צָא   אֶ|רֶץ

5

S C.1   **When is a syllable closed and when is it open?**

1)   Generally speaking, a syllable is closed when it ends with a consonant and open when it ends with a vowel or a vowel sound.[10]

?   Divide the words below into syllables and identify the syllables as open or closed:

11 קוּם   אֲדָמָה   מָלֵא   מֶלֶךְ   כְּלִי   קָמְתָ

2)   When a consonant has dagesh forte, it closes one syllable and begins the next: יְדַבֵּר syllabically is יְ דַב בֵּר Thus, how to demarcate the syllables in בּ is a problem.

3)   **Meteg** (a small vertical line written next to a vowel; it denotes an open syllable) causes a bit of a difficulty.

In a word such as אָכְלָה *she ate,* the meteg distinguishes the first qamats from qamats ḥatuf seen in אָכְלָה *food.* That is not the problem. The problem is whether in אָכְלָה there are two or three syllables. According to Gesenius, the "usual view" is that the meteg separates the syllables and the shewa is vocal (§9*u.*1*a*), but he goes on to explain in a later section (§16*i*) that Jewish grammarians do not consider the meteg to be opening the syllable. Thus the shewa is silent and the word has two syllables. Then there is the compromise position: shewa after meteg creates half a syllable.

S D   **There are two situations in which it is unclear whether a shewa is vocal or silent: when it is after a meteg and when shewa has made dagesh forte disappear What is the beginner, to do?**

Treat them as vocal and blame it on me. (For more detail see discussion on meteg in the paragraph just above, Vocalization D item 5 in the textbook, and Lesson 2:12.)

?   In the words below, identify the vocal shewas:

12 נִגְאַל   וַיַּעֲמֹד   יִשְׂרָאֵל   וְיִשְׁלְכוּ   פְּקַדְתִּי   יִתְּנוּ   אֲשֶׁר

---

[10] For example, both כָּה_ and ךָ_ are open. For more on the syllable, see Joüon, §27.

11 קָמְ תָ   כְּ לִי   מֶ לֶךְ   מָ לֵא   אֲ דָ מָה   קוּם

קָמְ תָ		כְּ לִי		מֶ לֶךְ		מָ לֵא		אֲ דָ מָה			קוּם
open	closed	open	open	closed	open	open	open	open	open	open	closed

12 אֲשֶׁר   יִתְּנוּ   פְּקַדְתִּי   וְיִשְׁלְכוּ   יִשְׂרָאֵל   וַיַּעֲמֹד   נִגְאַל

אֲשֶׁר	יִתְּנוּ	פְּקַדְתִּי	וְיִשְׁלְכוּ	יִשְׂרָאֵל	וַיַּעֲמֹד	נִגְאַל
אֲ	תְּ	not vocal	וְ לְ	not vocal	עֲ	not vocal

NOT SO PROPER READING EXERCISE

—◆—

Transliterate into English the following consonant-vowel combinations:

אִי אַם לֶרְנִיג טוּ רֶעְד הִבְּרוּ

_____

הוּא עֶז יוֹר פֵיבֹרֶט פְּרָפֶת

_____

מֶנִי סְטוּדֶנְץ קַם פְרַם אַל עוֹבֶר

_____

נוּע יֶרְק הֶז לָץ עֶב אֶבְּרִיתִינְג

_____

רָחֶל וָז בֶּרִי בְּיָתִיפוֹל

_____

דוּא יוּ נוּע גְרִיק אֶנְד אֶרֶמֶיִק

_____

מִי פְרֶנְדֶס אֶנְד עַי לָיְק הֶא אִיט פִּיצָה

_____

אֶסְתֶּר בִּיקֶם כְּבִין אֶפְשֶר וַשְׁתִּי

_____

סְטֵאיִנְג עַף אַל נָאיִת מֶקְס אָה פְּרֶשָׁן טָיִרד תָע נֶכְצַת דֵאי

_____

_____

מָי נֵיבּוֹר פְּלֶיז מָזִק עַת פוֹר אִי־אֶם

_____

_____

7

LESSONS

LESSON 1

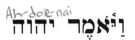

Ah-doe-nái

וַיֹּאמֶר יְהוָה

Genesis 3:13

§ 1.2   **What kind of grammatical significance does dagesh forte have?**

Many kinds, as you will see. Whenever you identify a dagesh as forte, you must determine what kind of information it is giving you about the word. In this lesson, you learned that its presence in a letter following **וְ** helps identify that letter as a prefix pronoun, the word as a verb, and the tense as past. In the next lesson, you will learn that its presence in the middle root letter of a verb helps identify the Pi`el stem. The third lesson will point out its function as denoting an assimilated letter, and so on.

§ 1.3   **Do all words, even prepositions, have three-letter roots?**

No, not all. The three-letter root is stressed because the standard academic dictionary, *The New Brown-Driver-Briggs-Gesenius Hebrew and English Lexicon*, commonly known as BDB, puts most words under actual or hypothetical triliteral roots. A few are listed as biliterals (two letters) or quadriliterals (four letters). Some root identification is controversial. This can be determined by looking at more than one lexicon. *The New Koehler-Baumgartner*, referred to here as K-B, is worth consulting for different concepts.

§ 1.3c   **What is the vav conversive converted from?**

There is a prefix form without vav conversive (see Verb Charts), which is most often translated in the future but can express incompleted action in any tense. So the vav conversive is converting the tense from future to past or from incompleted to completed action: **יֹאמֶר** *he will say* **וַיֹּאמֶר** *and he said*. Another name for the construction is "vav consecutive," which addresses sequence of actions.

§ 1.4a   **What do the various stems really do?**

Roughly speaking, when the system works ideally, **Qal** is basic: "I <u>broke</u> the dish"; **Nif`al** is passive (or reflexive): "I dropped the dish and it <u>broke</u>"; **Pi`el** is intensive: "I was so angry that I <u>smashed</u> the dish" or iterative: "I was so angry that I <u>kept breaking</u> dishes"; **Hif`il** causative, "I bumped into the food server and <u>made her break</u> the bloody dish,"etc. But the system is not always so neat, and there may be no obvious reason why a verb is in a particular stem. The stems, however, are morphologically distinct: a verb in the Qal will be formed differently from a verb in the Pi`el or Hif`il, etc.[1]

---

[1] For a brief overview, see excursus on The Verb (pp. 70–74) and the Glossary entries for each stem. For fuller discussions, see Gesenius §38–55; Joüon §40–59; and Waltke and O'Connor, chapters 20–28.

וַיֹּאמֶר יהוה

?

a) Which of the following could be vav conversive constructions?

וַיִּפְקֹד   יִפְקֹד   וַתִּמְלֹךְ   וַיֹּאכַל   וַנִּשְׁמֹר

b) In those that you picked, circle the root letters.

c) Of the letters that are left in those words, what is the function of the one that is not ו

_____

d) When a word begins with וֹ what three pieces of information is it giving you?

_____ **2**

---

2 a) The vav conversive constructions are   וַיִּפְקֹד וַתִּמְלֹךְ וַנִּשְׁמֹר

b) The roots are פקד מלך שמר

c) It is a prefix pronoun.

d) 1) The word is a verb. 2) The letter after the ו is a subject pronoun. 3) The verb is translated in the past tense.

12

LESSON 2

וַיְדַבֵּר אֱלֹהִים אֶל־מֹשֶׁה וַיֹּאמֶר אֵלָיו אֲנִי יהוה

Exodus 6:2

S 2.5   **Can one count on maqqef for anything?**

Beyond loss of accent (and even then, occasionally not), it is not a good idea. The maqqef will not necessarily distinguish one construction from another, a verb from a noun, or anything really useful like that.

§ 2.9   **Why does the word אֶל become אֵל when a suffix is added?**

That has to do with vowel changes in open and closed syllables. The preposition אֶל by it-self is a closed syllable (it ends in a consonant). When a suffix is added, as in אֵלָיו the א becomes an open syllable (it is also pretonic, for an explanation of which see **S 5.1c**); due to the vagaries of Hebrew, it needs a longer vowel. The י is another story. If the reasons do not interest you now, it will suffice to say that some prepositions have י before a suffix is added (two you know already are אֶל and עַל). If the reasons do interest you, see footnote.[1]

?   Write (without vowels):   on it _____   to him _____   not on him _____ [2]

---

[1] One possibility is that prepositions are derived from nouns. In the case of אֶל and עַל the third letter of the noun may have been ה Odd as it may seem, 3rd ה roots were originally 3rd י roots. The י of such roots reappears when an element, such as a suffix, is added to the word. Another possibility is that some prepositions take plural form when a suffix is added. This is seen in prepositions that exist as three strong letter enti-ties and take plural form before a suffix, e.g., אַחַר *behind* אַחֲרָיו *behind him/it* תַּחַת *under* תַּחְתָּיו *under him/it.* These three-letter prepositions are sometimes plu-ral before a noun. For example, Genesis 22:1 has אַחַר הַדְּבָרִים הָאֵלֶּה whereas Genesis 22:20 reads אַחֲרֵי הַדְּבָרִים הָאֵלֶּה Thus there is clear evidence for that position (Joüon, §103B, calls these pseudo-plurals), but the evidence may not apply to the origin of י in two-letter prepositions like אֶל and עַל For a full discussion of prepo-sitions, see Waltke and O'Connor, chapter 11.

[2]   on it עליו   to him אליו   not on him לא עליו

וַיְדַבֵּר אֱלֹהִים אֶל־מֹשֶׁה וַיֹּאמֶר אֵלָיו אֲנִי יהוה

S 2.10b   **Is word order significant in a noun sentence?**

Yes and no. יהוה אֲנִי and אֲנִי יהוה may mean the same thing, but depending on context, accents, and position in the verse, the emphasis would be on one or the other word.

S 2.12   **Is the shewa in וַיְדַבֵּר vocal?**

That is controversial. (See § **D**, but it won't help!) My opinion, derived from comparing texts from different manuscript traditions and from cantillating the text, is that it is vocal.

S 2.12.1   **Does the absence of dagesh forte in the prefix pronoun of וַיְדַבֵּר mean that וַיְדַבֵּר is no longer a vav conversive construction?**

No, it still is. Shewa can make dagesh forte disappear, which can make a construction such as vav conversive more difficult to identify.

?   a)   What does יהוה מֶלֶךְ mean? _____

   b)   What is the name of the construction? _____

   c)   Translate: עָלָיו _____

   d)   How is עָלָיו constructed similarly to אֵלָיו _____   3

?   When a suffix is added to a word or a word is made plural, the vowels of the word may change. Write the root portion of the words below as they appear in the vocabulary list (1–20).

4 בֵּיתוֹ _____ מַלְכּוֹ _____ בָּנִים _____ מְלָכִים _____ אַרְצוֹ _____

---

3 a)   יהוה מֶלֶךְ means **Adonai** (or **the Lord**) **is king.**

   b)   It is a noun sentence

   c)   עָלָיו means **on him** or **on it.**

   d)   They both have י before the suffix

4   בַּיִת   מֶלֶךְ   בֵּן   מֶלֶךְ   אֶרֶץ

14

LESSON 3

וַיֵּלֶךְ דָּוִד מִשָּׁם

1 Samuel 22:1

S 3.1   **In the word וַיֵּשֶׁב can the י be part of the root יֵשׁב**

According to the missing-letter "rule" in this section, the missing root letter for וַיֵּשֶׁב is
י so the root should be יֵשׁב and it is. But when a word begins with וַ and it is followed by
a letter containing dagesh forte, the letter containing the dagesh forte will be a prefix pronoun (1.3c). It cannot at the same time be a root letter. The י of the root יֵשׁב has elided
just as the ה of הָלַךְ did in וַיֵּלֶךְ This is confusing when the prefix pronoun is י and
the first root letter is also י Look at the 1st י Verb Chart (Chart D) and you will see that
when the prefix pronoun is ת (2 m. and f., sg. and pl.), א (1 c. sg.), or נ (1 c. pl.) potential ambiguity disappears.

?   Write the roots of the following words:

וַיֵּלֶךְ _____   וַתֵּצֵא _____   וַיֵּצְאוּ _____   וַיֹּאמֶר _____

וַתֵּדְעוּ _____   וַיִּקְרָא _____   וַתַּעַמְדוּ _____ [1]

S 3.3a   **Is there any truth to the rumor that the בגדכפת BeGaDKePHaT letters only
take dagesh lene?**

None at all! Any time those consonants are preceded by a full vowel, their dagesh is forte
and performing some significant grammatical function. Dagesh, whether lene or forte,
changes the pronunciation of פ פּ   כ כּ   ב בּ [2] Dagesh forte, in addition, makes
a grammatical point.

---

[1] וַיֵּלֶךְ←הלך   וַיֵּצְאוּ and וַתֵּצֵא ←יצא   וַיֹּאמֶר←אמר

וַתֵּדְעוּ ←ידע   וַיִּקְרָא ←קרא   וַתַּעַמְדוּ←עמד

[2] Geographic location and/or religious sensibility can affect pronunciation of ג ת and ד
with and without dagesh.

§ 3.3a.1   When dagesh is in the first letter of a word, is it lene or forte?

That is controversial. Gesenius, at §20c, says it is forte. Yeivin, #394–416, is not so sure. Considering that dagesh in the first letter of a word is phonetic and not grammatical, we will go with the not-so-sure opinion and consider it lene.

§ 3.3a.2   In Lesson 2 we learned that dagesh forte is not written in the י of וַיְדַבֵּר Is that an exclusive situation?

Unfortunately, no. וַיְדַבֵּר illustrates that shewa under a consonant needing a dagesh forte can make the dagesh disappear. In this particular example, the need is for dagesh forte in the prefix pronoun י as part of the vav conversive construction. (1.3b) A second situation: Dagesh may not be written when a consonant needing a dagesh forte is the last letter of a word, as in the preposition עַם *with*, derived from the root עמם However, when a suffix is added to עַם so that the "mem" is no longer the last letter, the doubling shows: עִמּוֹ *with him*. A third example: In the Pi'el prefix of צוה *command*, one sees יְצַוֶּה but with vav conversive, the ה is usually not written, making the middle root letter the final letter: וַיְצַו Consequently, it does not carry the dagesh. (Note: וַיְצַו is missing two dageshes forte. And finally, the gutturals + resh ר ע ח ה א rarely admit dagesh.

?   Identify every dagesh forte in the words below:

³ יִגְּשׁוּ אִשָּׁה כַּף פָּקַדְתִּי גִּבּוֹר בַּבַּיִת תָּסֵב הִנֵּה

§ 3.3a.3   Have we now learned everything there is to know about dagesh forte?

Of course not! There are some places in BHS where dagesh forte seems to appear after a composite shewa. That seems to be a peculiarity of the Leningrad manuscript on which BHS is based, for if one consults a printed text based on the Second Rabbinic Bible, one sees that in those suspect places there is either no dagesh or the previous vowel is full. Moreover, in a few cases, dagesh after a simple shewa is thought to be forte by some grammarians.

It does not help to solve the problem to know that Gesenius, at §12, footnote 1, writes that the Masoretes did not distinguish between dagesh forte and dagesh lene in terms of grammatical function, but used a dagesh where they considered that a letter had a sharp sound. The grammatical distinction is, apparently, a more recent concern.

All that said, we will stay with our identification and definition of dagesh forte for the duration of the course.

---

³ הִנֵּה תָּסֵב בַּבַּיִת גִּבּוֹר פָּקַדְתִּי כַּף אִשָּׁה יִגְּשׁוּ
    ↑   ↑   ↑   ↑   ↑   ↑

LESSON 4

וְלֹא־שָׁמַע הַמֶּלֶךְ אֶל־הָעָם

1 Kings 12:15

S 4.4b   **What is the special problem of segolate nouns?**

Nouns beginning with the pattern ֶ ◌ such as מֶלֶךְ and אֶרֶץ are a problem in the singular when a suffix is added because the first segol will become, usually, pataḥ ◌ַ (A class) or ḥireq ◌ִ (I class), and there is no way of knowing which vowel will appear until you see it.[1]

מַלְכּוֹ ← מֶלֶךְ   קִרְבּוֹ ← קֶרֶב

his king   king   *his inward part   inward part*

S 4.5b   **עַם in the vocabulary list has pataḥ, but הָעָם has qamets. Why?**

Preceded by the definite article, עַם regularly becomes עָם But it is a peculiarity of this word that without the definite article it is seen as either עַם or עָם regardless of accent.

S 4.5b.1   **Do vowels other than patah ◌ַ lengthen when a guttural or ר demands compensation for a needed dagesh forte?**

Yes. Ḥireq becomes tsere ◌ֵ ← ◌ִ

מִשָּׁם *from there*   but מֵאֶרֶץ *from a land*

↑ dagesh forte   ↑ compensation

?   Write in Hebrew:

the eye _____   the year _____   from David _____

from a father _____   the king _____   the one _____ [2]

---

[1] We are addressing only the most common and basic situations here. For in-depth coverage, consult Joüon §88 C or Gesenius §84a I.

[2] the eye   הָעַיִן   the year   הַשָּׁנָה   from David   מִדָּוִד

    from a father   מֵאָב   the king   הַמֶּלֶךְ   the one   הָאֶחָד

S 4.5b.2   **Does compensatory lengthening always occur when dagesh forte is needed in a guttural or ר**

No. א ע ר most usually demand compensation. ה and ח may not. In such cases, the vowel for the definite article remains pataḥ ַ e.g., הַחֹדֶשׁ *the month* (the doubling is considered to be "virtual"). (See **S 21.3a.1** for more detail.) There is another important thing to know about the definite article: **shewa can make dagesh forte disappear** (2.12.1). This can happen not only with a vav conversive construction but in any situation in which a consonant needs a dagesh forte, such as the definite article. So one might see הַלְוִים *the Levites* or הַלְוִים also *the Levites*.

LESSON 5

◆

דְּבַר־יְהוה אֲשֶׁר הָיָה אֶל־הוֹשֵׁעַ
Hosea 1:1

§ 5.1c   **When a word is in construct, are its vowel changes predictable?**

To an extent. Consider the word דָּבָר and why it becomes דְּבַר in construct with
יהוה Because both syllables of דָּבָר are distant from the accent—"distant" means two
syllables or more—both become shorter. The first syllable reduces from דָּ to דְּ because
it is open. The second syllable בָר shortens to בַר because it is closed.

§ 5.1c.1   **What are some common progressions of vowel shortening?[1]**

A   ָ   shortens to ְ ֲ or ַ

I   ֵ   shortens to ְ ֱ or ֶ

I   יִ יֵ originally long, do not change.[2]

U   וֹ and long וּ shorten to ְ[3] or in a closed, unaccented syllable to ָ

Diphthong   יַ֫ reduces to יְ   בַּ֫יִת ← בֵּית־

Diphthong   וָ֫ reduces to וֹ   מָ֫וֶת ← מוֹת־

§ 5.1c.2   **The vocabulary list shows that nouns such as יָד בֵּן דָּבָר have different vowels in construct, in the plural, and when a suffix is added. Why?**

The vowel changes have to do with distance from the accent and whether a syllable is
open or closed. Look at a few examples of the word דָּבָר

---

[1] Note: not all vowels will shorten when a noun is in construct. Vowels that are already
short like those in אֶרֶץ and עַם stay that way, and vowels that are "originally long" as
in אִישׁ may not shorten. To know whether a vowel was "originally long" one has to
know the history of the word.

[2] Unless one knows the history of a word, one cannot know when ִ and ֵ are in the
category of short vowels or are defectiva spellings of the long vowels יִ and יֵ.

[3] ָ can be long or short.

19

דְּבַר־יהוה אֲשֶׁר הָיָה אֶל־הוֹשֵׁעַ

דְּבָרִים *words*　　דְּבָרוֹ *his word*　　דְּבַר־ *word of*　　דָּבָר *word*

We can see that the vowel one syllable distant from the accent tends to behave differently from a vowel that is two (or more) syllables distant from the accent. These positions are specifically described: the accented syllable is **tonic,** the syllable before it is **pretonic,** and the one before that is **propretonic.**

?　In the words below, identify each syllable as tonic, pretonic, or propretonic:

אֱלֹהִים　　מֹשֶׁה　　יְהוּדָה　　עִיר　　שָׁמַע[4]

For nouns (and verbs with a suffix), the tendency is for the pretonic vowel to be long and the propretonic vowel to be short. This is referred to as

pretonic lengthening; propretonic reduction

§ 5.1c.3　**Can we see some examples of pretonic lengthening and propretonic reduction for all the vowels?**

Yes. <u>Note</u>: These progressions apply to nouns, adjectives, and verbs with a suffix.

A　 ָ ָ when pretonic, is always the longer vowel ָ

דָּבָר ← דְּבָרִים

In דְּבָרִים pretonic בָ stays long; propretonic דְּ reduces from דָ

I　 ִ ֵ when pretonic, will be the longer vowel ֵ if the propretonic vowel can reduce:

זָקֵן ← זְקֵנִים

In זְקֵנִים (*elders*) pretonic קֵ is long; propretonic זְ reduces from זָ

I　 ִ ֵ if the propretonic vowel cannot reduce, then the pretonic vowel will:

מִזְבֵּחַ ← מִזְבְּחוֹת

In מִזְבְּחוֹת (*altars*) propretonic מִ can't reduce,[5] so pretonic בֵ reduces to בְּ

---

[4]　יְהוּדָה דָה tonic, הוּ pretonic, יְ propretonic　　עִיר tonic　　שָׁמַע מַע tonic, שָׁ pretonic

　אֱלֹהִים הִים tonic, לֹ pretonic, אֱ propretonic　　מֹשֶׁה שֶׁה tonic, מֹ pretonic

[5]　Its reduction would lead to there being two vocal shewas in a row. That problem is discussed in **S 14.3.1.**

U ן ֹו (like **I**) will be long pretonically if the propretonic vowel can reduce:

$$\text{גְּדֹלִים} \leftarrow \text{גָּדוֹל}$$

In גְּדֹלִים (*big*) pretonic ֹד is long; propretonic גְּ reduces from גָּ

U ֹו ֹו (like **I**) if the propretonic vowel cannot reduce, the pretonic vowel will:

$$\text{יִקְטְלֵם} \leftarrow \text{יִקְטֹל}$$

In יִקְטְלֵם (*he will kill them*) propretonic יִ can't reduce, so pretonic טֹ reduces to טְ

? Using the vowel changes described above as models, translate:

the kings _____   his name _____   the name of his son _____

the word _____   his word _____   the people of Israel _____ **6**

? Name four situations that can move vowels away from the accent:

_____ **7**

? Write the following construct chains (use of maqqef is optional):

the land of the king _____   the word of the king _____

the man of God _____   the city of David _____

a son of a priest _____   the house of Israel _____ **8**

S 5.2 **Does shewa under the first letter of a noun always indicate a change from the absolute?**

It usually does, but not always. Some nouns have shewa under the first root letter because that is how they are formed, for example, אַיִל *ram* כְּלִי *vessel* פְּרִי *fruit*. (It is thought, though, that these initial shewas were originally full vowels because vocal shewas are considered to be a result of shortening.)

---

6 the kings הַמְּלָכִים   his name שְׁמוֹ   the name of his son שֶׁם־בְּנוֹ

the word הַדָּבָר   his word דְּבָרוֹ   the people of Israel בְּנֵי־יִשְׂרָאֵל

7 1) addition of a suffix   2) plural endiNG   3) maqqef   4) construct state

8 the land of the king אֶרֶץ הַמֶּלֶךְ   the word of the king דְּבַר הַמֶּלֶךְ

the man of God אִישׁ (הָ) אֱלֹהִים   the city of David עִיר דָּוִד

a son of a priest בֶּן־כֹּהֵן   the house of Israel בֵּית־יִשְׂרָאֵל

S 5.2.1   **Is "compensatory lengthening" the reverse of "shortening"?**

No. Compensatory lengthening occurs when a consonant cannot take a dagesh it needs, for example, in forming the definite article or the Pi'el. In such cases, patah ַ under the letter before may lengthen to qamats ָ and hireq ִ may lengthen to tsere ֵ

The longer vowel is "compensating" for the absent dagesh. This change will take place even when a syllable is distant from the accent. For example, in the phrase מֵעַם־הָאָרֶץ *from the people of the land*, the vowel tsere ֵ three syllables from the accent, is compensating for the fact that the עֵ of עַם cannot take a dagesh to represent the assimilated נ of the preposition מִן (3.4b)

S 5.2.2   **When the absolute and construct look the same, how can one distinguish between a construct chain and a noun sentence?**

Context can help, for example, מֶלֶךְ יִשְׂרָאֵל makes more sense translated as *the king of Israel* than *a king is Israel* or *Israel is king* (but of course, you never know), and אִישׁ מֶלֶךְ is more likely to mean *a man is a king* than *a man of a king*.

Another thing to bear in mind is the "rules" of the construct chain. יהוה מֶלֶךְ would be *Adonai is king*, a noun sentence, since the word in construct is not supposed to carry a mark of definiteness and יהוה being a proper noun is definite.

S 5.2.3   **Does word order matter in a construct chain?**

Yes! The construct must come before the absolute. מֶלֶךְ הַבַּיִת could only be *the king of the house*. It could <u>not</u> be *the house of the king*.

?   Identify each phrase below as a noun sentence or a construct chain:

עַם הָאָרֶץ _____   יַד־יהוה _____   יהוה אֱלֹהִים _____

דָּוִד מֶלֶךְ _____   יהוה אֶחָד _____   בֶּן דָּוִד _____ 9

S 5.3a   **Why does אֲשֶׁר have a composite shewa under the א**

Composite shewas are used under gutturals and sometimes ר when a vocal shewa is needed. A shewa under the first letter of a word is always vocal.

עַם הָאָרֶץ9 const. chain   יַד־יהוה const. chain   יהוה אֱלֹהִים noun sent.

דָּוִד מֶלֶךְ noun sent.   יהוה אֶחָד noun sent.   בֶּן דָּוִד const. chain

דְּבַר־יהוה אֲשֶׁר הָיָה אֶל־הוֹשֵׁעַ

Glossary Review

Absolute

Composite shewa

Construct chain

Dagesh lene

Form

Guttural letter

Number

Person

Prefix form

Proper noun

Radical

Segolate noun

Stem

Suffix

Torah

Verb

Vulgate

BeGaDKePHaT

Consonant

Dagesh

Defectiva

Full vowel

Maqqef

Object pronoun

Plene

Prepositional phrase

Qal

Root

Semitic language

Subject

Syllable

Vav consecutive

Vowel class

Cognate

Construct

Dagesh forte

Definite article

Gender

Noun sentence

Particle

Possessive pronoun

Pronoun

Quiescent

Relative pronoun

Septuagint

Subject pronoun

Triliteral

Vav conversive

Vowel letter

LESSON 6

וַיְּבֹאוּ עַד־הַיַּרְדֵּן הוּא וְכָל־בְּנֵי יִשְׂרָאֵל

Joshua 3:1

S 6.1   **How can both a prefix and an affix form have a subject component at the end of a verb and still be distinct?**

An affix form has a subject pronoun only at the end of a verb.

A prefix form must have a subject component at the beginning of a verb and may, in addition, have a complementary component at the end.

S 6.1a   Under what root letters would you look up the following words?

?   קָבַר _____   וַיָּמֻתוּ _____   וַיִּשְׁלַח _____   וַיֵּדְעוּ _____

       [1]וַתֵּשֶׁב _____   וַתָּבֹא _____   וַתֵּלֶךְ _____

T or F   כּוֹל and כָּל־ are pronounced the same way.[2]

S 6.3a   **Circle each qamats ḥatuf in the words below. Note that a meteg (a little line usually to the left of a vowel) means that that syllable is open.**

?   [3]בָּרוּךְ   יִשְׂרָאֵל   כָּל־   אֶחָד   שָׁמְרוּ   שָׁמְרוּ   אָכַל

S 6.6   **How is a prefix pronoun (before the root) or an affix pronoun (after the root) different from an independent subject pronoun?**

An independent subject pronoun is not physically attached to a word. For example: in שָׁמַע *he heard*, the subject, "he," is part of the form. But in שָׁמַע הוּא *He* heard or *that man heard*, or even *that man, he heard* הוּא is an independent subject pronoun. In that case, the subject is actually stated twice. But remember also that the subject of the verb alone is 3 m. sg. and will be translated "he" only by default. There could be a noun or proper noun as a subject as in שָׁמַע הַמֶּלֶךְ *the king heard*.

---

[1] קָבַר ← קבר   וַיָּמֻתוּ ← מות   וַיִּשְׁלַח ← שלח   וַיֵּדְעוּ ← ידע

    וַתֵּשֶׁב ← ישב   וַתָּבֹא ← בוא   וַתֵּלֶךְ ← הלך

(For hollow roots, וֹ ו or י could be the middle letter. Here, though, the middle letter should be obvious because both בוא and מות are vocabulary words.)

[2] True. See 6.3a.

[3] In שָׁמְרוּ and כָּל־ the qamats is a qamats ḥatuf and pronounced like וֹ

24

LESSON 7

וַיִּתֵּן אַבְרָהָם אֶת־כָּל־אֲשֶׁר־לוֹ לְיִצְחָק

Genesis 25:5

S 7.2c   **Is there a difference between the prepositions** אֶל **and** לְ

Not definitively, although אֶל tends to suggest motion toward. Also אֶל can be an independent word, but לְ cannot. With a suffix—and using the 3 m. sg. suffix for our example—לוֹ is more flexible in meaning than אֵלָיו   Both can mean *to him*

אָמַר לוֹ   *he said to him*   דִּבֶּר אֵלָיו   *he spoke to him*

But only לוֹ indicates possession:

עֶבֶד לוֹ   *he has a servant (a servant to him).*

?   Translate:

1 לֹא לוֹ הָעֶבֶד   _____

2 לוֹא נָתַן לוֹ עַבְדּוֹ   _____

3[1] לוֹא נָתַן אֵלָיו עַבְדּוֹ   _____

T or F   In the word וַיִּתֵּן the dagesh forte in the תֵּ may indicate the Pi'el stem.[2]

---

[1] 1. the servant was not his (not to him the servant)   2. and 3. he didn't give him his servant

[2] False. It can represent only the assimilated נ of the root. See 7.1a.

25

LESSON 8

וַיָּדְעוּ כִּי־שְׁמִי יהוה

Jeremiah 16:21

S 8.1b **ו at the end of a word often indicates a m. pl. subject. Does it interchange with וֹ or וֹ**

No. וֹ__ or וֹ__ appended to a word can mean *his* or *him*. וּ__ cannot.

? State the function of the ו at the end of each word below:

וַיֵּצְאוּ _____   עַמּוֹ _____   הָיוּ _____   יָדָיו _____

עֵינוֹ _____   עֵינָיו _____   דִּבְּרוּ _____   פָּנָיו _____ 1

S 8.1c **Could the י in יָדְעוּ be a prefix pronoun?**

No. In Lesson 3 we discussed 1st י verbs (granted, with vav conversive) in the prefix form, an identifying characteristic of which is the vowel tsere __ under the prefix pronoun; such is not the case here. In Lesson 6 we saw a hollow verb in the prefix (again with vav conversive), and it did have qamats under the prefix pronoun: וַיָּבֹא But a hollow verb in the prefix has וֹ וֹ or וֹ__ (or at least a U or I class vowel) between its strong letters; again not the case with יָדְעוּ So, since the י is not וֹ and there is no U or I class vowel in the middle of the word, the only choice left is that the י is a root letter and along with the vowel qamats __ is indicating Qal hollow affix. When י is the first letter of a word, you have to determine whether it is a root letter or a prefix pronoun.

S 8.3 **In the word שְׁמִי how does one determine whether the base word is שֵׁם or שָׁם**

Process of elimination. שָׁם *there* with a suffix would not make sense.

---

¹וַיֵּצְאוּ verb indicator   עַמּוֹ possessive suffix   הָיוּ verb indicator   יָדָיו possessive suffix

עֵינוֹ possessive suffix   עֵינָיו possessive suffix   דִּבְּרוּ verb indicator   פָּנָיו possessive suffix

26

S 8.3.1   **If ‍ֽ_ is the 1 c. sg. suffix on a singular noun, what is "my" on a plural noun?**

The 1 c. sg. suffix on a plural noun is ‍ַי   So דְּבָרַי *my word*   דְּבָרִי *my words.*

?   Translate:

בְּנוֹ _____	בְּנִי _____	בְּנַי _____
בָּנָיו _____	בְּנֵי _____	² בָּנִים _____

1   לֹא יָדַע וְלֹא עָשָׂה _____

2   שֵׁם־הָעִיר חֶבְרוֹן _____

3   הוּא הָאִישׁ _____

4   בֵּית הַמֶּלֶךְ _____

5   וְרָאָה אֶת־עִירוֹ _____

6   וְנָתְנוּ לְדָוִד אֶת הַכּוֹל _____

7   הִנֵּה בְנִי _____

8   מִיָּדוֹ _____

9   לָקַח אַבְרָהָם אֶת־יִצְחָק _____

10   זֶה הַבַּיִת _____

11   וַיֵּצֵא מִן הָאָרֶץ וַיָּמָת _____

12   וַיָּבֹאוּ כָל־עַם הָאָרֶץ _____

13   וַיִּתְּנוּ לִי בַיִת _____

14   וְלוֹא יָצָא _____

15   וַיֵּצֵא _____

16   וְיָצָא _____

2	his son בְּנוֹ	my son בְּנִי	my sons בָּנַי
	his sons בָּנָיו	sons of בְּנֵי	sons בָּנִים

וְיָדְעוּ כִּי־שְׁמִי יהוה

17 יוֹם אֶחָד _____

18 וַיָּשָׁב _____

19 וַיֵּשְׁבוּ _____

20 וְיֵשְׁבוּ _____

21 דִּבֶּר דָּבָר _____

22 וַיֵּשֶׁב יְהוּדָה עִם מְלָכִים _____

23 עֵינֵי כָּל־יִשְׂרָאֵל עָלָיו _____

24 אֶת־פְּנֵי־יהוה לֹא רָאָה _____

25 ³ כִּי שָׁלַח הָאָב אֶת־בְּנוֹ אֶל הָעִיר _____

3

1 he didn't know and he didn't do	13 and they gave me a house
2 the name of the city is Hebron	14 and he did not go out
3 he/that is the man	15 and he went out
4 the house of the king	16 and he will go out
5 and he will see his city	17 one day (day one)
6 and they will give to David everything (the whole)	18 and he returned
7 behold my son	19 and they returned
8 from his hand	20 and they will dwell
9 Abraham took Isaac	21 he spoke a word
10 this is the house	22 and Judah dwelled with kings
11 and he went out from the land and he died	23 the eyes of all Israel are on him
12 and all the people of the land came	24 he did not see the face of the Lord
	25 because the father sent his son to the city

LESSON 9

וְהֵם לֹא יָדְעוּ כִּי שֹׁמֵעַ יוֹסֵף

Genesis 42:23

S 9.3 **Can the word following a participle, such as יוֹסֵף be the object of the participle?**

Yes it could. If that were the case here, one would expect יוֹסֵף to be preceded by אֵת (though a DDO does not have to be marked by אֵת). But before thinking "object," one must first identify a subject for the participle. Unless a subject is implied, it must be supplied, so here, יוֹסֵף must be the subject. The more context one has, the more obvious that kind of decision would be.

T or F In the sentence "singing can help pass the time," *singing* is a participle.[1]

S 9.5 **9.5a is very confusing. Is more explanation possible?**

Worth a try. Hollow verbs in the affix form are difficult because their hollow vowel does not appear. This means that in the affix of בוֹא the vowel וֹ will not show, nor will the וֹ in שׁוּב or the י in שִׂים[2] The two consonants left take—in the third person—the usual Qal affix vowel, $_\bar{\ }$ Thus בָּא *he came* (or *he entered*), שָׁב *he returned*, שָׂם *he put*. That's the first point.

The Qal active participle of a hollow does not take the usual ḥolem after the first root letter. It keeps the qamats. Therefore, the 3 m. sg. affix and the m. sg. participle look alike.[3] (Plurals are not ambiguous. The affix would end in וּ and the participle with יִם בָּאוּ can only be *they came*, and בָּאִים can only be some yet-to-be-determined *"they" coming*.)

---

[1] False. A participle cannot stand for the action of a verb in the abstract. (In Hebrew the infinitive fills that function.)

[2] Indeed, a number of grammarians believe that hollows are biconsonantal and not formed from three-letter roots at all. However, BDB lists them in the infinitive form in order to show three letters. Other verbs are listed under the 3 m. sg. Qal affix. The vocabulary list follows BDB convention.

[3] The feminine singular has the same ambiguity, but we are not there yet!

29

Back to the singular and 9.5a

Example 1: אֵין יוֹצֵא וְאֵין בָּא

These are two parallel segments: each has two words, each segment begins with the same word, and the verbs are opposite or complementary actions. Since in the first phrase יוֹצֵא is clearly a participle, then בָּא in the second is likely to be one too.

Example 2: In the case of בָּא אָנֹכִי | בָּא must be a participle because בָּא as an affix would be 3 m. sg. *he came,* and the subject here is first person. (Reminder: participles do <u>not</u> have person; they have only gender [m. or f.] and number [sg. or pl.].)

Example 3: Only the participle can take the definite article (because participles take the accoutrements of nouns; the affix does not) so הַבָּא would be _____

All this being said, without the definite article to identify the form, there are times when it may be hard to know whether affix or participle is intended.

LESSON 10

—

וַיָּבֹא אֶל־אָבִיו וַיֹּאמֶר אָבִי וַיֹּאמֶר הִנֶּנִּי

Genesis 27:18

§ 10.1b **What is the real reason for the י between אָב and the suffix ? Does not י after a masculine noun denote the plural?**

To answer the second part first: yes, י after a masculine noun does denote the plural. אָב is irregular. Its root is actually אבה (The one other noun similar to אָב in that it, too, behaves similarly is אָח *brother*, and its root is אחה) The consonant ה in the third root letter position was historically י That ancient י is seen in place of the present ה when any element is added to a word, in this case a suffix. Many nouns that come from 3rd ה roots end in י such as פְּרִי *fruit* from the root פרה *be fruitful* (you haven't seen any of these nouns yet), but the noun אָב loses the last letter in its formation (as does אָח). One could say, then, that the י seen when a suffix is added is not extra; the noun without the final י is defectiva.[1]

§ 10.2d **How do the accents work?**

The accents are musical phrases that have three functions: they show where each word is accented, they divide a verse into phrases, and they make the text beautiful. The accents are of two types: conjunctive and disjunctive. Disjunctive accents may be used independently, but a conjunctive accent needs a disjunctive to close a phrase.

The accent is usually on the last syllable (this is called milra). It may be on the second to last syllable (called mil`el). In most words in the Bible, the accent is written just to the left of the accented syllable. However, some accents are pre-positive (always on the first consonant) or post-positive (on the last consonant). In those cases one has to know the grammar to know where to accent the word. Shewa, simple or composite, never gets the accent. On ☉ אב you can hear four of the readings cantillated according to the accentual system.

S 10.2d.1 **Is there a difference between accent and pause?**

Sort of. The accent or tone syllable is the place where the word is stressed in pronunciation. Pause refers only to the strongest disjunctive accents, so it is, in a sense, a subcate-

---

[1] <u>Note</u>: When the suffix of אָח or אָב is יִ *my*, an extra י is not added.

31

gory of accent. The strongest disjunctive accents are: silluq, which looks exactly like a meteg ַ (8.1e) but is always the accent for the last word of a verse, atnaḥ ֑ which appears in every verse except for some very short ones; and zaqef qaton, the accent that looks like a shewa on top of a letter: בֿ

S 10.2d.2 What does pause do?

It frequently changes the quantity or quality of vowel.

$$אֶחָד ← אֶחָד: \qquad תֹּאכַל ← תֹּאכֵל \qquad פֶּסַח ← פָּסַח$$

S 10.2d.3 How else are syllables, vowels, and accents related?

1) For a syllable to be accented, it must have a full vowel. Stated in reverse: a syllable with shewa ְ or composite shewa ֱ ֲ ֳ will never be accented.

2) An important bit of information about syllables, vowels, and accents concerns identification of qamats ḥatuf (qamats ָ in a closed, <u>unaccented</u> syllable). Its identity is important because it represents a short וֹ or וּ and is most helpful in identifying some forms of hollow verbs, Qal imperatives, and infinitives with suffixes, Hof`als, etc. Examples:

qamats ḥatuf ↓

יָקוּם *he will arise* (prefix form), but וַיָּקָם *and he arose* [2] (pronounced va-ya-kom), wherein the syllable קָם preserves the medial U class vowel in יָקוּם as qamats ḥatuf.

qamats ḥatuf ↓

שָׁמוֹר (infinitive construct: (*to*) *guard*) but שָׁמְרוֹ (infinitive construct + suffix) *his guarding* (pronounced shome-<u>ro</u>) again preserves the U class vowel of the infinitive even though that vowel is now under the first syllable.

3) Maqqef usually makes the word before it lose its accent; thus the qamats in כָּל־ is in a syllable that is closed by the ל and unaccented because of the maqqef and so is qamats ḥatuf. כָּל־ provides an especially nice example of qamats ḥatuf because it is easy to see that it is a derivative of כּוֹל

---

[2] The syllable קָם in וַיָּקָם is both closed and unaccented.

32

4) Meteg is very useful in distinguishing between qamats and qamats ḥatuf. Its presence means the syllable is open. Unfortunately, it is not always used. שָׁמְרוּ *they guarded* is a good example; there is no meteg but the initial qamats is an A class vowel. This absence of the meteg in the combination ָ ְ when meteg would in fact be useful can be especially frustrating because it requires one to know grammar well and sometimes even something about the history of a word to know whether the qamats is an A class vowel or a qamats ḥatuf.

?

Identify qamats ḥatuf in the words below:

³ בִּזְכָרֵנוּ הָאָדָם דָּמוֹ וּבְכָל־ טָרָף וְאָסְפָּה וַיָּמָת

---

³ וַיָּמָת וְאָסְפָּה טָרָף וּבְכָל־ דָּמוֹ הָאָדָם בִּזְכָרֵנוּ
↑ ↑ ↑

33

LESSON 11

וַיֵּצְאוּ לָלֶכֶת אַרְצָה כְּנַעַן וַיָּבֹאוּ אַרְצָה כְּנָעַן

Genesis 12:5

S 11.2   **Why does** ל **in front of** לֶכֶת **have the vowel qamats** ◌ָ **and not shewa** ◌ְ **?**

לֶכֶת the infinitive of הָלַךְ is formed as a segolate noun (**S 4.4b**), so the accent is on the first syllable. The preposition ל being pretonic, is lengthened to לָ (**S 5.1c**)

S 11 2a   **Do all 1st** י **infinitives follow the pattern of** לֶכֶת

They all end in ת and ◌ֶ ◌ֶ is the usual pattern for 1st י infinitives, but gutturals can affect the vowel pattern: דַּעַת ← יָדַע and צֵאת ← יָצָא for example.

But רֶדֶת ← יָרַד   לֶדֶת ← יָלַד   שֶׁבֶת ← יָשַׁב and so on.

S 11.3   **Why the patah under the** א **of** אַרְצָה

אֶרֶץ is an A class segolate noun. (**S 4.4b**) Directive or locative ◌ָה is a suffix that causes the A vowel to show, just as any other suffix would: אַרְצוֹ for example.

LESSON 12

◄——►

וַיַּרְא כָּל־הָעָם וַיִּפְּלוּ עַל־פְּנֵיהֶם

1 Kings 18:39

S 12.1   **Can we review some of the weak roots in the vav conversive?**

?   Of course. Below are weak roots taken from words 1–100 in the vocabulary list. Give the root of each (the pertinent Lessons are 3, 6, 7, 12). Answers in footnote.[1]

וַיְהִי _____	וַיַּעַשׂ _____	וַיָּבֹאוּ _____
וַיִּחְיוּ _____	וַיִּתְּנוּ _____	וַיֵּלֶךְ _____
וַיִּרְאוּ _____	וַיֵּשֶׁב _____	וַיֵּשֶׁב _____
וַיֵּשְׁבוּ _____	וַיֵּצְאוּ _____	וַיֵּדַע _____
וַיַּעֲלוּ _____	וַיָּמָת _____	וַיִּשְׂאוּ _____

T or F   וַיִּגְּשׁוּ could be from a 3rd ה root. _____[2]

?   Which of the words below are from the root יֹשׁב

שָׁבִים יוֹשֵׁב יָשְׁבוּ וַיֵּשֶׁב וַיָּשָׁב וַיֵּשְׁבוּ וַיֵּשֶׁב וַיָּשָׁב לָשֶׁבֶת[3]

S 12.1.1   **Do the missing-letter rules always work?**

Not always, but often enough to begin with them. If the rule should fail, go to a different weak root. For example, a word that looks like a 1st י might be a 3rd ה

---

[1]
היה	עשה	בּוֹא
חיה	נתן	הלךְ
ראה	ישב	שׁוּב
שׁוּב	יצא	ידע
עלה	מות	נשׂא

[2] False. The dagesh forte in the ג signifies that a נ has been assimilated, so the root is נָגַשׁ
For the missing-letter rules to kick in, the letter <u>really</u> has to be missing.

[3]   יוֹשֵׁב יָשְׁבוּ וַיֵּשֶׁב וַיָּשָׁב לָשֶׁבֶת

S 12.4 Could we see some examples of the 3 m. pl. suffix with the ◻ָ__ spelling?

אַרְצָם *their land*   דְּבָרָם *their word*   יָדָם *their hand*   כֻּלָּם *all of them*

? Translate:

הַמִּשְׁפָּט _____   מִשְׁפָּטֵי _____   מִשְׁפָּטִי _____

מִשְׁפָּטוֹ _____   מִשְׁפָּטֵיהֶם _____   מִשְׁפָּטָם _____

מִשְׁפָּטִים _____   מִשְׁפָּטַי _____   מִשְׁפָּטָיו _____

[4] אֲבִיהֶם _____   אָבִיו _____   אָבִי _____

---

[4]
my judgment	מִשְׁפָּטִי	judgments of	מִשְׁפָּטֵי	the judgment	הַמִּשְׁפָּט
their judgment	מִשְׁפָּטָם	their judgments	מִשְׁפָּטֵיהֶם	his judgment	מִשְׁפָּטוֹ
his judgments	מִשְׁפָּטָיו	my judgments	מִשְׁפָּטַי	judgments	מִשְׁפָּטִים
my father	אָבִי	his father	אָבִיו	their father	אֲבִיהֶם

LESSON 13

וַיֹּאמֶר הִנְנִי כִּי קָרָאתָ לִי

1 Samuel 3:8

S 13.5   **Why are verbs conjugated in the order third, second, first person?**
Because the 3 m. sg. sets the pattern for the conjugation.

§13.5.1   **The 3 m. sg. פָּקַד is the model on which the other PGNs build, but they don't all follow its _ _ vowel pattern. Why?**

The most obvious variation from the פָּקַד pattern is the 2 m.pl. פְּקַדְתֶּם and 2 f. pl. פְּקַדְתֶּן which have shewa under the first root letter (instead of the landmark qamats ָ) due to propretonic reduction. (Remember: The accent is tonic, the syllable before the accent is pretonic, and the one before that is propretonic.) That takes care of that variant.

The other change from the פָּקַד pattern is in 3 f. sg. פָּקְדָה and the 3 c. pl. פָּקְדוּ[1] which do not have pataḥ ַ under the second root letter. Pataḥ is the usual vowel when the second syllable is closed; shewa is the usual vowel when the syllable is open.

Putting all this together, you get the following regularities for the Qal affix: The vowel under the first root letter will be _____ except for the 2 m. pl. and the 2 f. pl. where it reduces to _____ When the second syllable is open its vowel will be _____ ; when it is closed, the vowel will be _____[2]

?   The following are verbs in the Qal affix. Using the information just above, fill in the remaining vowels:

עזבנו שמרתם שאל הרגה שמחתי קברתן בטחו [3]

---

[1] For information on the meteg, see **S 10.2d.1**, item 4.

[2] The vowel under the first root letter will be ָ except for the 2 m. pl. and 2 f. pl. where it reduces to ְ   When the second syllable is open, the vowel will be ְ when it is closed, the vowel will be ַ

בָּטְחוּ קָבַרְתֶּן שָׂמַחְתִּי הָרְגָה שָׁאַל שְׁמַרְתֶּם עֲזָבְנוּ [3]

37

S 13.6a   **Why do 3rd א verbs have qamats ָ as the second vowel of the Qal affix?**

The change from pataḥ ַ to qamats ָ (קָרָא instead of פָּקַד e.g.) occurs because the א creates an open syllable. Open syllables, especially when accented, tend to have long vowels. Qamats is a longer A class vowel than pataḥ, though both are considered to be short.

S 13.6b   **Why do verbs that begin with a guttural take composite shewa instead of simple shewa in the 2 m. and f. pl. Qal affix?**

One sees הֲלַכְתֶּם instead of פְּקַדְתֶּם for example because gutturals and sometimes ר use a composite shewa (instead of simple shewa) as their vocal shewa. Since shewa is vocal when it is under the first letter of a word, a guttural in that position will require a composite shewa.

?   The affix pronouns are:

3 m. sg. _____	3 c. pl. _____
3 f. sg. _____	
2 m. sg. _____	2 m. pl. _____
2 f. sg. _____	3 f. pl. _____
1 c. sg. _____	1 c. pl. _____ **4**

?   Write the following verbs in the Qal affix:

3 c. pl.	נתן _____	1. c. sg.	לקח _____
3 f. sg.	הלך _____	2 f. sg.	קרא _____
2 m. pl.	ידע _____	2 f. pl.	אמר _____
2 m. sg.	ישב _____	1 c. pl.	אכל _____ **5**

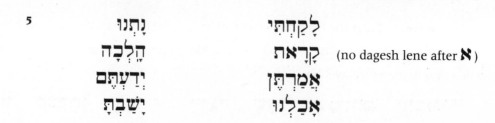

4

3 m. sg. nothing added	3 c. pl. ⸗וּ
3 f. sg. ⸗ָה	
2 m. sg. ⸗תָּ	2 m. pl. ⸗תֶּם
2 f. sg. ⸗תְּ	2 f. pl. ⸗תֶּן
1 c. sg. ⸗תִּי	1 c. pl. ⸗נוּ

5

נָתְנוּ	לָקַחְתִּי
הָלְכָה	קָרָאת (no dagesh lene after א)
יְדַעְתֶּם	אֲמַרְתֶּן
יָשַׁבְתָּ	אֲכַלְנוּ

LESSON 14

כִּי־תִשְׁמֹר אֶת־כָּל־הַמִּצְוָה הַזֹּאת לַעֲשֹׂתָהּ

Deuteronomy 19:9

S 14.1   **Why is there no dagesh in the ת of תִשְׁמֹר**

This is the complement of a phenomenon discussed at **S 17.3b**, the euphonic dagesh. But to answer the question: When a word beginning with a BeGaDKePhaT letter, such as תִשְׁמֹר follows a word that ends with an open syllable—here כִּי—and is closely connected to it by a maqqef or a conjunctive accent, it frequently does not get a dagesh.

S 14.1.1   **Could we review "tense" for the affix and prefix with and without ו**

For now, we will list the most basic possibilities:

הָלַךְ	affix	past tense or completed action: *he went*
וְהָלַךְ	affix with ו	future tense: *and he will go*
וְהָלַךְ	affix with ו	less often, repeated action in the past: *and he used to go*
וְהָלַךְ	affix with ו	least often in Biblical Hebrew, past tense: *and he went*
יֵלֵךְ	prefix	future or incomplete action: *he will go*
וְיֵלֵךְ	prefix with plain ו	future or incomplete action: *and he will go*
וַיֵּלֶךְ	prefix with vav conversive	past tense or completed action: *and he went*

S 14.2c   **Can an attributive adjective modify the noun in construct in a construct chain?**

Yes, but the adjective would have to come after the whole chain:

attributive adjective   absolute   construct

↓   ↓   ↓

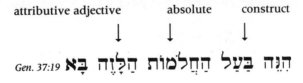

Gen. 37:19   הִנֵּה בַּעַל הַחֲלֹמוֹת הַלָּזֶה בָּא

Behold, <u>this master</u> of dreams is coming

14.3   Match each final ה‎ to its function or functions:

1) הֶ֫   a) הֵ directive

2) הַ   b) 3 f. sg. affix pronoun

3) הָ   c) 3 f. sg. object suffix

                 d) 3 f. sg. possessive suffix

                 e) f. sg. noun endiNG[1]

§ 14.3.1 Why is the preposition לְ of לַעֲשֹׂתָהּ vocalized לַ rather than לְ

The answer to that question brings us to the notorious **rule of shewa**.

The rule of shewa states that there cannot be two vocal shewas in a row (two shewas, yes, but not two <u>vocal</u> shewas. עֲבָדְךָ has two shewas in a row; only the second is vocal.) לְ + עֲשֹׂתָהּ would have two vocal shewas in a row. Why? _____

_____ **2**

The problem of there being two vocal shewas in a row is almost exclusive to a word beginning with an attached preposition or וֹ

1) When the combination is shewa + composite shewa, for example, לְ + אֱכֹל the first vocal shewa becomes the full vowel of the composite shewa. (This is called "mirroring.")

לְ + אֱכֹל→לֶאֱכֹל   לְ + עֲמֹד→לַעֲמֹד

There are two exceptions:

לְ + אֱלֹהִים→לֵאלֹהִים   and   לְ + אֱמֹר→לֵאמֹר

1a) The same resolution takes place if the word begins with וֹ

וֹ + אֱכֹל→וֶאֱכֹל   וֹ + עֲמֹד→וַעֲמֹד

---

[1] 1 b and e; 2 c and d; 3 c and d.

[2] לַ is vocal because it is under the first letter of the word. עֲ is vocal because it is the second shewa in a row. (It is written as a composite shewa because it is vocal under a guttural letter.)

2) When a word begins לְ‎ then לְ‎ ← לִ‎ ← לְ‎

לְ‎ + שְׁמוֹ ← לִשְׁמוֹ *for his name*

2a) But when a word begins וְ‎ then וְ‎ + ← וּ‎

וְ‎ + רְאֵה ← וּרְאֵה *and see!*

2b) And when a word begins וְיְ‎ then וְיְ‎ + ← וִי‎

וְ‎ + יְרוּשָׁלַ͏ִם ← וִירוּשָׁלַ͏ִם

? Rewrite the words below according to the rule of shewa:

³ כְּעֵלַת _____ בִּכְלִי _____ וְלְעוֹף _____ פְּקִדוּ _____ וְיְהִי _____

S 14.3.2 **What other factors can affect the vocalization of attached prepositions or וְ**

One was already discussed in **S 11.2**. To refresh: If the preposition or וְ is pretonic, then

often לְ‎ ← לָ‎ or וְ‎ ← וָ‎

Just regarding וְ when the word begins with a BuMP letter בּ מ פּ initial וְ‎ → וּ

וּבַחֹדֶשׁ הַשֵּׁנִי *and in the second month*

וּמִלְאוּ אֶת־הָאָרֶץ *and fill the land*

וּפָרַצְתָּ *and you will burst forth*

Finally, remember that vav conversive is a special construction with its own rules for vocalization. (1.3b and 14.5a.)

? Write the correct vowel for the conjunction וְ in the words below:

⁴ וְיהוּדָה וְאָכַל וָמֵת: וַיִּשְׁמַע וְשָׁמַרְתִּי וּשְׁמִי וּבֵן וַיֵּלֶךְ

S 14.3a **How are the Qal infinitives construct for 3rd ה and 1st י verbs different?**

Both infinitives lose their weak letter and both end in ת
But 3rd ה infinitives end in ‎וֹת‎ 1st י infinitives do not.

---

³ כְּעֵלַת בִּכְלִי וְלְעוֹף פְּקִדוּ וְיְהִי

⁴ וְיהוּדָה וְאָכַל וָמֵת: וַיִּשְׁמַע וְשָׁמַרְתִּי וּשְׁמִי וּבֵן וַיֵּלֶךְ

?

Give the root of each of the following infinitives:

לִרְאוֹת⁵ _____ לֶכֶת _____ לֶדֶת _____ צֵאת _____ הֱיוֹת _____

S 14.5   **Is there an easy way to recognize a prefix form without vav conversive?**

Not as easy as with vav conversive. But only four consonants can possibly be prefix pronouns: י א ת נ⁶ so that restricts the options. Prefix vowel patterns are important because they show the vowel pattern for the imperative, participle, and infinitive in most stems.

S 14.5.1   **The Qal prefix form has two main patterns, יִפְקֹד and יִשְׁלַח Is there any way of knowing which verbs will follow which pattern?**

Not precisely. The יִפְקֹד pattern is most common, but third gutturals, having a strong affinity for pataḥ _ tend to follow the pattern of יִשְׁלַח Also I and U class verbs (17.6a) often follow the יִשְׁלַח pattern, but there is no hard and fast rule. (The 3 m. sg. prefix and prefix with vav conversive is given in the vocabulary list.)

S 14.5.2   **The interior vowel pattern is not consistent even within the paradigm. Why?**

One constant (for the strong verb) is ḥireq _ under the prefix pronoun, with one exception: the 1 c. sg. prefix pronoun א which takes segol: אֶפְקֹד The main inconsistency within the paradigm is that the theme vowel, ḥolem וֹ or pataḥ _ after the second root letter, is, in some PGNs, reduced to shewa _ As in the Qal affix, when the second syllable is open, it takes shewa; when it is closed, it takes the theme vowel of the paradigm—in the case of the Qal prefix, either ḥolem or pataḥ.

תִּשְׁ|לְ|חִי   יִשְׁ|לַח   תִּפְ|קְ|דוּ   תִּפְ|קֹד|נָה
open ↑   closed ↑   open ↑   closed ↑

?

Given the above information, fill in the vowels for the following prefix form verbs whose theme vowel is ḥolem:

תלכד   אשרף   יפתחו   תשמרנה   נשפט⁷

לִרְאוֹת←ראה   לֶכֶת←הלך   לֶדֶת←ילד   צֵאת←יצא⁵
הֱיוֹת←היה

⁶ Try one of these the mnemonics for the prefix pronouns: ANTY אנתי or YeNTA ינתא

⁷ נִשְׁפֹּט תִּשְׁמֹרְנָה יִפְתְּחוּ אֶשְׂרֹף תִּלְכֹּד

? Now fill in the vowels for the following verbs whose theme vowel is pataḥ:

8 תגאלו   תלבשנה   אזבח   תבחרי   יכבד

S 14.5.3   **Prefix complements are confusing. Any tips here?**

Only one singular PGN (2 f.) תִּפְקְדִי has a prefix complement, and only one plural (1 c.) נִפְקֹד does not.

? Write the following verbs in the Qal prefix. Those that are third guttural have pataḥ as their theme vowel:

3 m. sg.	מלך _____	1 c. pl.	שלח _____	
3 f. pl.	מלך _____	2 m. pl.	קרא _____	
2 m. sg.	שמע _____	3 m. pl.	פקד _____	
1 c. sg.	פקד _____	2 f. sg.	מלך _____	
3 f. sg	שלח _____	2 f. pl.	שלח _____	9

---

8   יְכְבַּד   תִּבְחֲרִי   אֶזְבַּח   תִּלְבַּשְׁנָה   תִּגְאֲלוּ

9   יִמְלֹךְ   נִשְׁלַח

תִּמְלֹכְנָה   תִּקְרָאוּ

תִּשְׁמַע   יִפְקְדוּ

אֶפְקֹד   תִּמְלְכִי

תִּשְׁלַח   תִּשְׁלַחְנָה

LESSON 15

◆

וַיֹּאמֶר חִזְקִיָּהוּ אֶל־יְשַׁעְיָהוּ טוֹב דְּבַר־יהוה אֲשֶׁר דִּבַּרְתָּ

Isaiah 39:8

S 15.2 **Are attributive adjectives and predicate adjectives always distinguishable?**

Not always. A predicate adjective usually precedes the noun, but it may follow. So טוֹב אִישׁ could be, and usually would be, *a good man*—attributive use of טוֹב it follows the noun and agrees in gender (m.), number (sg.), and definiteness (both אִישׁ and טוֹב are indefinite). טוֹב אִישׁ could also mean *a man is good*—predicate use of טוֹב even though a predicate adjective usually precedes the noun. When the noun and adjective do not agree in definiteness, then the adjective must be predicate.

טוֹב הָאִישׁ can only be *the man is good*. A noun and a predicate adjective form a construction that is really the same as a noun sentence (2.10b).

S 15.4a **Is the Pi̇'el affix of middle א ה ח ע ר a problem?**

It can be. It does make sense that because the middle letter does not take dagesh the vowel under the first root letter goes from hireq ◌ִ to tsere ◌ֵ for example, בֵּרֵךְ instead of דִּבֵּר It is a whole other matter to recognize it when you see it! And what's more, compensation is not always required. When the middle consonant is ה or ח (and sometimes ע) there is no dagesh and no compensatory lengthening: נִהַג *he led*.

? Write the Pi̇'el affix of the following roots:

2 m. sg.	דבר	_____	1 c. pl.	שלח	_____
3 f. sg.	עבר	_____	2 f. pl.	ברך	_____
3 m. pl.	ברך	_____	1 c. sg.	נהג	_____ 1

1

2 m. sg.	דִּבַּרְתָּ		1 c. pl.	שִׁלַּחְנוּ
3 f. sg.	עִבְּרָה		2 f. pl.	בֵּרַכְתֶּן
3 m. pl.	בֵּרְכוּ		1 c. sg.	נִהַגְתִּי

44

S 15.5   **How dependable a Pi'el indicator is shewa under the prefix pronoun?**

Very. That is good news and bad news. The good news is that you can count on that shewa as a distinguishing sign of the Pi'el prefix no matter what the middle consonant. The bad news is that shewa under the prefix pronoun is not exclusive to the Pi'el. For example, וַיְהִי *and it happened*, is a 3 m. sg. Qal prefix form with vav conversive of a 3rd ה root.

?   Write the Pi'el prefix of the following roots:

1 c. pl.	הלך	_____	1 c. sg.	ברך	_____
3 f. pl.	שמע	_____	3 f. sg.	ילד	_____
2 f. sg.	נשא	_____	2 m. pl.	דבר	_____ **2**

?   When does compensatory lengthening occur? _____ **3**

?   What are two vowel progressions that show compensatory lengthening? _____ **4**

Hint   If at this point in the course—or at any other time, for that matter—you are feeling over-whelmed by verbs and grammar, here is an idea: Keep up with the lessons the class is doing but go back to the beginning of the book for a programmed review. Day one, review carefully Lessons 1–3; day two, Lessons 4–6, day three, Lessons 7–10, and so on. Do the same with vocabulary.

?   **Quiz:** Most of the words below are verbs, but not all are.

Translate and where gender and/or number are not clear, clarify. For example, designate "you" as sg. or pl. and as m. or f. and "they" as m. or f.

	B		A	
_____	לִרְאוֹת	_____	קִדַּשְׁתֶּם	1
_____	אֹהֳלֵיהֶם	_____	נָשָׂאתִי	2
_____	אֲדַבֵּר	_____	אֶמְלֹךְ	3
_____	תִּשְׁמְעִי	_____	וְעָבַרְתָּ	4

2

1 c. pl.	נְהַלֵּךְ	1 c. sg.	אֲבָרֵךְ	
3 f. pl.	תְּשַׁמֵּעְנָה	3 f. sg.	תְּיַלֵּד	
2 f. sg.	תְּנַשְּׂאִי	2 m. pl.	תְּדַבְּרוּ	

3 When a letter needing a dagesh forte cannot take one, the vowel before it may be lengthened.

4 Pataḥ ַ lengthens to qamats ָ and ḥireq ִ lengthens to tsere ֵ

45

A		B	
5	אֵין מַיִם	וַיִּבֶן	
6	קָרְאוּ	יְרַדְתֶּן	
7	רוּחִי	יָרֵא	
8	מְצָאתֶם	וַתָּשֶׂם	
9	אָכַלְנוּ	אַתָּה הָאִישׁ	
10	תַּעֲמְדוּ	וַנָּמָת	
11	עֵינֵיהֶם	וּמְצָאתֶם	
12	תִּשְׁלַחְנָה	תָּקוּמוּ	
13	יָשְׁבָה	וְלָקַחְנוּ	
14	לֵב גָּדֹל	תֵּצְאוּ	
15	נְבָרֵךְ	דַּעַת	

5

	B	A
1	to see	you (m. pl.) sanctified (Pi'el)
2	their (m. pl.) tents	I lifted
3	I will speak	I will rule
4	you (f. sg.) will hear	and you (m. sg.) will cross over
5	and he built	there is no water
6	you (f. pl.) went down	they (c. pl.) called
7	he was in awe	my wind/spirit
8	and she/you (m. s.g) put	you (m. pl.) found
9	you are the man!	we ate
10	and we died	you (m. pl.) will stand
11	and you (m. pl.) will find	their (m. pl.) eyes
12	you (m. pl.) will arise	you/they (f. pl.) will send
13	and we will take	she dwelled
14	you (m. pl.) will go out	a big heart
15	to know	we will bless (Pi'el)

וַיֹּאמֶר חִזְקִיָּהוּ אֶל־יְשַׁעְיָהוּ טוֹב דְּבַר־יהוה אֲשֶׁר דִּבַּרְתָּ

Glossary Review

Accentual system

Adverb

Assimilation

Collective noun

Compound subject

Definite direct object

Feminine

Indefinite

Intransitive

Object of preposition

Passive voice

Phrase

Predicator of existence

Strong verb

Transitive

Voice

Active voice

Affix form

Attributive adjective

Common (gender)

Conjunction

Direct object

Furtive pataḥ

Independent pronoun

Lexicon

Object pronoun

Pause

Pointing

Quiescent

Syntax

Ultima

Weak verb

Adjective

Antecedent

Clause

Compensatory lengthening

Context

Direct speech

Heavy ending

Indirect object

Meteg

Participle

PGN

Predicate adjective

Relative clause

Tone

Vav reversive

Word order

LESSON 16

—

וַיִּפֹּל יוֹסֵף עַל־פְּנֵי אָבִיו וַיֵּבְךְּ עָלָיו וַיִּשַּׁק־לוֹ:

Genesis 50:1

S 16.1a **What are the pitfalls of 1st) verbs in the Qal prefix?**

The main thing to be careful of is assigning the dagesh to the right function and not re-flexively thinking, "dagesh forte, middle root letter → Pi`el." <u>That is not always the case.</u> First you must determine the root. If the dagesh is representing the ) of the root, it cannot also be representing the Pi`el. (<u>Note</u>: In 1st) as in the strong verb, the Qal prefix has two main patterns as illustrated by יִפֹּל and יִשַּׁק)

? Identify the Pi`el prefix forms among the following:

¹נֹהֵג   נִנְהַג   תְּבָרְכוּ   יְנַשֵּׁק   יִשַּׁק   יִנָּפֵל   יִפֹּל

S 16.3a **Will 3rd ה prefix forms with vav conversive in the Qal often look like 1st י**

Just often enough to consider 3rd ה as a root if tsere ֵ under the prefix pronoun does not yield a 1st י root.² Without vav conversive, the 3rd ה of the root will be written except in the jussive mood. (42.1)

S 16.3a.1 **Can one assume that whenever a consonant drops out of a word the consonant is a root letter?**

The disappearing letter won't be an affix or a prefix pronoun or a prefix complement, but elements other than root letters can drop out of words. The letters most commonly not written are) which tends to assimilate and ה which tends to elide. 12.4 pointed out that the suffix הֶם or הֶם can lose its ה when the word to which the suffix is attached ends in a consonant: יָדָם *their hand* instead of יָדְהֶם for example. In Genesis 22:3 you

---

¹ נִנְהַג   תְּבָרְכוּ   יְנַשֵּׁק   יִנָּפֵל

² Tsere ֵ under the prefix pronoun can be the indicator of the Nif`al prefix of first gutturals, יֵאָמֵר for example, but the rest of the vowel pattern distinguishes these Nif`als from Qal prefix forms that have tsere under the prefix pronoun as in a 1st י → יֵצֵא or some 3rd ה verbs → וַיֵּבְךְּ

וַיִּפֹּל יוֹסֵף עַל־פְּנֵי אָבִיו וַיֵּבְךְּ עָלָיו וַיִּשַּׁק־לוֹ:

saw the elision of a ה twice: once in the Hif`il prefix וַיַּשְׁכֵּם and then in the ה of the definite article in בַּבֹּקֶר You haven't seen a direct example of a נ assimilating except as a root letter, but it can under other circumstances (as part of a Nif`al preformative, for example).

T or F Both the first and final נ of נתן assimilate before a consonant.[3]

? Write the Qal affix for: she gave _____ I gave _____ we gave _____
they gave _____ he gave _____ you (m.pl.) gave _____ [4]

---

[3] True. See 16.6. But not before a vowel. In נָתְנָה *she gave*, the נ stays. In נָתַתָּ *you gave*, it assimilates.

[4] she gave	נָתְנָה	I gave	נָתַתִּי	we gave	נָתַנּוּ
they gave	נָתְנוּ	he gave	נָתַן	you gave	נְתַתֶּם

LESSON 17

◆

יהוה לִי לֹא אִירָא מַה־יַּעֲשֶׂה לִי אָדָם:

Psalms 118:6

§ 17.2 **How many kinds of 1st ׳ verbs are there?**

In fact, there are three kinds, and things become quite complicated since the categories are not neatly separated.

1) 1st ׳ verbs that lose the ׳ in the Qal prefix and have tsere _ under the prefix pronoun. The most common of these are:

ירד *go down*   ישב *sit/dwell*   ילד *bear*   ידע *know*   יצא *go out*   הלך *go/walk*

2) 1st ׳ verbs that keep the ׳ of the root in the Qal prefix and have ḥireq _ under the prefix pronoun:

ירא *be in awe*   ישן *sleep*   יעף *be weary*   יעץ *advise*   יטב *be good*

ירש *inherit*   יבש *be dry*   יקץ *wake up*   ישר *be upright*

In these verbs, if the ׳ is not written, it will be represented by a meteg: יִרְאוּ instead of יִירְאוּ for example. (Alas, on rare occasions, even the meteg may be missing, but the vowel under the prefix pronoun will remain ḥireq _)

Because of the history of 1st ׳ verbs, these, that is, the ones like יִרָא that keep the ׳ of the root in the Qal prefix, can really be subdivided into two classes. There are those that were originally 1st ו which letter reasserts itself in the Nif`al and Hif`il. Example, נוֹרָא m. sg. Nif`al participle of יָרֵא *awesome*, shows the root ׳י←ו[1] The rest, which are only a few, are genuine 1st ׳ keeping that initial ׳ throughout the stem system.

---

[1] All the verbs of the first category, that is, the ירד type, were originally 1st ו so in those the ו will regularly appear in the Nif`al and Hif`il.

50

3)   A small group of 1st **י** roots having **צ** as a second root letter resemble 1st **נ**

Example **יִצֹק** *he will pour* looks as if the root is **נצק** Sometimes these 1st **יצ** roots

do not have the dagesh forte in the middle root letter, so one will also see **יִצֹק**

(Although **יצא** begins with **יצ** it is not in this category.)

For full coverage of 1st **י** verbs, see Joüon, § 74–77.

§ 17.3b   Is there more information on the euphonic dagesh?

This dagesh, which goes by a number of names—euphonic, dirimens, and conjunctive being three—is quite common and poorly understood.[2] It works like this: When a word ending in an open syllable has maqqef (e.g., **מַה־**) or a conjunctive accent and is followed by a word beginning with a non-BeGaDKePhaT letter, then the initial letter of the second word will usually have a dagesh.

Conversely, when a word with the conditions just mentioned (open syllable, conjunctive relationship) is followed by a BeGaDKePhaT letter, that letter will <u>not</u> have a dagesh, for example, **וַיְהִי־בֹקֶר** (Gen. 1:5).

S 17.6   What features are common to the conjugation of A , I, and U class verbs in the Qal affix?

1)   In the 3 m. sg. each class shows its identifying vowel.

?   Fill in the vowels:

	A	I	U
3 m. sg.	פקד	כבד	קטן [3]

2)   In the 3 f. sg. and 3 c. pl., the class vowel does not appear. (See **S 13.5** paragraph 2.)

?   Fill in the vowels:

	A	I	U
3 f. sg.	פקדה	כבדה	קטנה
3 c. pl.	פקדו	כבדו	קטנו [4]

---

[2] For more information, see Gesenius § 20.2.*c–g*

[3]	3 m. sg.	פָּקַד	כָּבֵד	קָטֹן
[4]	3 f. sg.	פָּקְדה	כָּבְדה	קָטְנָה
	3 c. pl.	פָּקְדוּ	כָּבְדוּ	קָטְנוּ

———

3) In the second and first persons, A stays A; but I → A;[5] U stays U.[6]

? Fill in the vowels:

	A	I	U
sg. 2 m.	פקדת	כבדת	קטנת
2 f.	פקדת	כבדת	קטנת
1 c.	פקדתי	כבדתי	קטנתי
pl. 2 m.	פקדתֹם	כבדתֹם	קטנתֹם
2 f.	פקדתֹן	כבדתֹן	קטנתֹן
1 c.	פקדנו	כבדנו	קנטנו [7]

S 17.6 a–d For זָקֵן *be old* and שָׁכֹל *be bereaved* write the following in the Qal:

?

1 c. sg. affix	_____	_____
f. sg. participle	_____	_____
f. pl. participle	_____	_____
3 f. sg. affix	_____	_____
2 m. sg. prefix	_____	_____ [8]

———————

[5] Tsere __ often becomes pataḥ __ in a closed syllable in the interior of a word.

[6] In the 2 m. pl. and 2 f. pl. the U class vowel is expressed as qamets ḥatuf.

[7]

	A	I	U
sg. 2 m.	פָּקַדְתָּ	כָּבַדְתָּ	קָטֹנְתָּ
f.	פָּקַדְתְּ	כָּבַדְתְּ	קָטֹנְתְּ
1 c.	פָּקַדְתִּי	כָּבַדְתִּי	קָטֹנְתִּי
pl. 2 m.	פְּקַדְתֶּם	כְּבַדְתֶּם	קְטָנְתֶּם
2 f.	פְּקַדְתֶּן	כְּבַדְתֶּן	קְטָנְתֶּן
1 c.	פָּקַדְנוּ	כָּבַדְנוּ	קָטֹנּוּ

[8]

1 c. sg. affix	זָקַנְתִּי	שָׁכֹלְתִּי
f. sg. participle	זְקֵנָה	שְׁכֹלָה
f. pl. participle	זְקֵנוֹת	שְׁכֹלוֹת
3 f. sg. affix	זָקְנָה	שָׁכְלָה
2 m. sg. prefix	תִזְקַן	תִשְׁכֹּל

52

S 17.7.3 **To what vowel class does the verb אָהַב belong?**

אהב *love*, has two patterns A: אָהַב and I: אָהֵב Its participle is formed from the A pattern: אֹהֵב There is not a consistent or strict categorization of "stative" verbs in Hebrew. (See Joüon § 40–41.)

LESSON 18

שְׁמַע יִשְׂרָאֵל יהוה אֱלֹהֵינוּ יהוה אֶחָד:

Deuteronomy 6:4

S 18.1a   **Are Qal imperatives as easy as they seem?**

The difficulty of Qal imperatives—indeed, of all imperatives—is related not to their formation; it is simple enough to take off the prefix pronoun from the second person prefix form. The difficulty is in recognizing them.

תִּשְׁמֹר←שְׁמֹר   תִּשְׁמְרִי←שִׁמְרִי   תִּשְׁמְרוּ←שִׁמְרוּ   תִּשְׁמֹרְנָה←שְׁמֹרְנָה

f. pl.   m. pl.   f. sg.   m. sg.

Notice that when the prefix pronoun is taken off the 2 f. sg. and the 2 m. pl. the resulting word begins with two shewas. This cannot stand because both shewas are now vocal: Shewa under the שׁ is vocal because _____ (S **D**) and under מ it is vocal because _____ (S **D**). (In the prefix form, the first shewa is closing a syllable so it is silent and only the second is vocal.) The most common way this problem is resolved is _____ (S **14.3.1**)

?   Identify the form of each word below:

_____ שָׁמַע   _____ שֹׁמֵעַ   _____ תִּשְׁמַעְנָה   _____ שְׁמַעְתֶּן

_____ שׁוֹמְעִים   _____ שִׁמְעִי   _____ תִּשְׁמְעוּ   _____ שִׁמְעוּ [1]

S 18.1b   **What is the explanation for the composite shewa in אֱמֹר**

The 2 m. sg. Qal prefix form is תֹּאמַר in which form the א is quiescent. But when the prefix pronoun is removed making א the first letter, it must have a vowel; that vowel will be a shewa, which will be vocal because it will be under the first letter of the word. However, since א is a guttural, it cannot use a simple shewa as its vocal shewa. So the question becomes: Which composite shewa will it take? Most gutturals have an affinity for pataḥ

---

[1] affix   שָׁמַע   participle   שֹׁמֵעַ   prefix   תִּשְׁמַעְנָה   affix   שְׁמַעְתֶּן

   participle   שׁוֹמְעִים   imperative   שִׁמְעִי   prefix   תִּשְׁמְעוּ   imperative   שִׁמְעוּ

under them and before them, but **א** especially in the first position prefers segol. Therefore, the composite shewa in this case is ֱ To illustrate the point with a different guttural, we will use עמד The m. sg. imperative of הַעֲמֹד is עֲמֹד

S 18.3b   אֱלֹהֵי is the form אֱלֹהִים takes when the suffix נוּ ֵ is added. **Does this mean that all m. pl. nouns look just like the construct form when they take a suffix?**

No. The vowel before the suffix is not always tsere ֵ *His God* would be אֱלֹהָיו The י of the plural will be there but the vowel before it depends on the consonant with which the suffix begins. One could say that the form of the noun to which a suffix is added is the construct form, but the vowels may not be the same as those of the word when it is part of a construct chain.

S 18.5   **Are attributive adjectives always definite?**

No. They can be either definite or indefinite. It depends on the definiteness or indefiniteness of the noun being modified by the adjective: A definite noun will be modified by a definite attributive adjective, an indefinite noun by an indefinite attributive adjective.

?   Translate into Hebrew:

that land _____   his good father _____

a great (big) nation _____   these words _____ **2**

T or F   Predicate adjectives are never definite.**3**

?   Translate into Hebrew:

the big man _____   the man is big _____

a big man _____   the big man of the land _____ **4**

---

2 that land הָאָרֶץ הַהִיא   his good father אָבִיו הַטּוֹב (his father, the good one)

a great (big) nation גּוֹי גָדוֹל   these words הַדְּבָרִים הָאֵלֶּה

3 True.

4 the big man הָאִישׁ הַגָּדוֹל   the man is big גָדוֹל הָאִישׁ or הָאִישׁ גָדוֹל or
הָאִישׁ הוּא גָדוֹל

a big man אִישׁ גָדוֹל   the big man of the land אִישׁ־הָאָרֶץ הַגָּדוֹל

55

LESSON 19

◆

וְאָמַרְתָּ דַּבֵּר יהוה כִּי שֹׁמֵעַ עַבְדֶּךָ

1 Samuel 3:9

S 19.2a

?

Review: Using the root שׁבר *break,* write the following in Hebrew:

m. sg. Qal participle _____		2 m. pl. Qal prefix _____	
1 c. sg. Qal prefix _____		m. sg. Qal imperative _____	
m. sg. Pi`el imperative _____		1 c. pl. Qal affix _____	
3 f. pl. Pi`el prefix _____		1 c. sg. Pi`el affix _____ **1**	

S 19.5   **When a word is "in pause," are vowel changes predictable?**

The description in the lesson covers the most common changes. Be on the lookout for these changes at the atnaḥ ◌ the silluq ◌ the zaqef qaton ◌ and sometimes the revia ◌ For a full discussion of vowel changes in pause, see Gesenius § 29 *i–w.*

---

1 m. sg. Qal participle	שׁוֹבֵר	2 m. pl. Qal prefix	תִּשְׁבְּרוּ
1 c. sg. Qal prefix	אֶשְׁבֹּר	m. sg. Qal imperative	שְׁבֹר
m. sg. Pi`el imperative	שַׁבֵּר	1 c. pl. Qal affix	שָׁבַרְנוּ
3 f. pl. Pi`el prefix	תְּשַׁבֵּרְנָה	1 c. sg. Pi`el affix	שִׁבַּרְתִּי

LESSON 20

———◆———

וַיִּקְרָא פַרְעֹה אֶל־מֹשֶׁה וַיֹּאמֶר לְכוּ עִבְדוּ אֶת־יהוה

Exodus 10:24

S 20.1   In the lesson sentence, the initial פ of פַרְעֹה does not have dagesh. Why? See **S 17.3b**.

S 20.6a   Give the roots of the following imperatives:

?   _____ רֵד   _____ שְׂאִי   _____ דְּעוּ   _____ שְׁבוּ

    _____ שֵׁבְנָה   _____ רְאוּ   _____ עֲשִׂי   _____ תֵּן¹

?   Write the imperatives of the verbs below:

    _____ תְּדַבֵּרְנָה   _____ תְּדַבְּרוּ   _____ תְּדַבְּרִי   _____ תְּדַבֵּר²

?   Circle each word below that is an imperative and note whether it is Qal or Pi`el:

    לַמֵּד   לְמַד   לִמְדוּ   בָּרְכִי   בָּרְכוּ   תִּכְבְּדִי   שְׁמַע³

?   Why does the ע in עִבְדוּ in the lesson sentence have a composite shewa?

    _____ 4

---

¹   רֵד →יָרַד   שְׂאִי → נָשָׂא   דְּעוּ → יָדַע   שְׁבוּ → שׁוּב

    שֵׁבְנָה →יָשַׁב   רְאוּ → רָאָה   עֲשִׂי → עָשָׂה   תֵּן → נָתַן

²   דַּבֵּרְנָה   דַּבְּרוּ   דַּבְּרִי   דַּבֵּר

³   לַמֵּד Pi`el    לִמְדוּ Qal    בָּרְכִי Pi`el   שְׁמַע Qal

⁴ Because, being under the first letter of a word, it is vocal and it is under a guttural letter. See **S 18.1b**.

57

LESSON 21

———

וַיִּקַּח יִשְׂרָאֵל אֵת כָּל־הֶעָרִים הָאֵלֶּה וַיֵּשֶׁב יִשְׂרָאֵל
בְּכָל־עָרֵי הָאֱמֹרִי

Numbers 21:25

S 21.1　　T or F　לקח is the only 1st ל that acts like a 1st י[1]

S 21.3a　　עִיר **is f. noun but its pl. is** עָרִים　**What gender are its adjectives and verbs?**

Feminine. The construct and absolute endings are masculine, but the word is not.

?　　Write:

the evil city _____　　　　the cities will fall _____

the cities of Judah _____　　the city has fallen _____ [2]

S 21.3a.1　　**Can one know whether the definite article before a guttural will be** הַ **,** הָ **or** הֶ

Before ע and א it is usually הָ

Before ח and ה it is usually הַ　If it is pretonic it may be הֶ

But when it is propretonic, whatever the guttural, it will usually be הֶ

———————————

[1] False.　לָקַח is the only 1st ל that acts like a 1st נ

[2] the evil city　　　הָעִיר הָרָעָה　　　　the cities will fall　　　תִּפֹּלְנָה הֶעָרִים

　　the cities of Judah　עָרֵי יְהוּדָה　　　　the city has fallen　　נָפְלָה הָעִיר

58

LESSON 22

לֹא־תִקַּח אִשָּׁה לִבְנִי מִבְּנוֹת הַכְּנַעֲנִי אֲשֶׁר אָנֹכִי יֹשֵׁב בְּאַרְצוֹ

Genesis 24:37

S 22.4 ‫וֹת‬ is the ending for f. pl. nouns and 3rd ‫ה‬ infinitives. How can one distinguish?

If a word shows three letters before the ‫וֹת‬ as in אֲדָמֹות the endiNG can only be signifying a f. pl. noun. If the body of the feminine noun has only two letters, that may be a problem. For example, בְּנוֹת can mean *daughters* and also *to build*. Context helps.

? Identify the following as a f. pl. noun, adjective, participle, or 3rd ‫ה‬ infinitive:

עֲלוֹת _____	רְאוֹת _____	נְפָשׁוֹת _____
חֲרָבוֹת _____	חֲיוֹת _____	גְּדֹלוֹת _____
עֲלוֹת¹ _____	מֵאוֹת _____	שָׁבוֹת _____

? Translate the following phrases:

the big cities _____ the city is big _____

the king of the land _____ the sword consumed _____

and she took water _____ take (m.) the good land _____²

---

¹ f. pl. noun נְפָשׁוֹת infinitive רְאוֹת infinitive עֲלוֹת

 f. pl. adjective גְּדֹלוֹת infinitive חֲיוֹת f. pl. noun חֲרָבוֹת

 f. pl. participle שָׁבוֹת f. pl. noun מֵאוֹת f. pl. noun/participle עֲלוֹת

² the big cities הֶעָרִים הַגְּדֹלוֹת the city is big גָּדְלָה הָעִיר

 the king of the land מֶלֶךְ הָאָרֶץ the sword consumed אָכְלָה הַחֶרֶב

 And she took water וַתִּקַּח מַיִם take the good land קַח|קְחוּ אֶת הָאָרֶץ הַטּוֹבָה

S 22.4a **How can one distinguish between a f. sg. noun and a 3 f. sg. affix, since both end in הָ**

Sometimes vowel patterns will help. מַלְכָּה would have to be the noun *queen* because the verb *she ruled* would be מָלְכָה (qamats under the first root letter being the sign of the Qal affix). There are other confusions, however. שָׁנָה is the f. noun *year*. It can also be a 3 m. sg. affix of a 3rd ה verb, *he changed;* yet קָמָה *she got up* is a f. sg. affix of a hollow root. There is no way to remove all potential ambiguities. Knowing vocabulary helps a lot, and context helps, too.

S 22.4a.1 **How can one recognize a f. sg. noun in construct? The ת ending is confusing.**

It is, but a reliable conversion is that final f. הָ becomes ת whenever an "element" is added. In a construct chain, the word(s) in construct cannot stand alone; the element added is the word in the absolute. A suffix is another element that would cause final feminine הָ to become ת One must remember to think backward when a final ת does not seem to be the end of a word as learned. (You will learn in Lesson 26 that "final feminine הָ becomes ת" occurs in verbs, too.)

? Translate:

one city _____   the war of David _____

his evil _____   the year of the war _____

a good year _____   a great evil _____ **3**

3

one city	עִיר אַחַת	the war of David	מִלְחֶמֶת־דָּוִד
his evil	רָעָתוֹ	the year of the war	שְׁנַת־הַמִּלְחָמָה
a good year	שָׁנָה טוֹבָה	a great evil	רָעָה גְדֹלָה

LESSON 23

אֶת־הָאָ֫רֶץ אֲשֶׁר־יהוה אֱלֹהֵיכֶם נֹתֵן לָכֶם וִירִשְׁתֶּ֫ם
אֹתָהּ וִישַׁבְתֶּם־בָּהּ

Deuteronomy 11:31

S 23.2a   When וְ←וִ is a meteg always there as in וִירִשְׁתֶּ֫ם in the lesson sentence?

When the entity is a verb, usually, but when a noun, usually not. For fuller coverage of the rule of shewa, especially regarding initial וֹ see **S 14.3.1**.

23.2b   T or F   1) At the end of a word הָ __ = הֹ __   2) הָ __ = הָ֫ ___ [1]

S 23.2b.1   Fill in the vowels for the following signs of the DDO plus suffix:

?   אֹתִי   אֶתְהֶן   אֹתוֹ   אֹתְךָ   אֶתְכֶם   אֹתָהּ   אֹתָ֫נוּ [2]

---

[1] 1) True. Both represent the 3 f. sg. suffix. 2) False הָ֫ is a f. sg. noun endiNG or a 3 f. sg. verb in the affix. הָ is the 3 f. sg. suffix.

[2] אֹתִי אֶתְהֶן אֹתוֹ אֹתְךָ אֶתְכֶם אֹתָהּ אֹתָ֫נוּ

LESSON 24

———

אֲנִי וְהָאִשָּׁה הַזֹּאת יֹשְׁבֹת בְּבַ֫יִת אֶחָד

1 Kings 3:17

S 24.5a   **Can יֹשְׁבוֹת be translated as either a noun or a verb?**

Yes. One has to decide whether to imbue a particular participle with a stronger verbal or nominal sense. In the lesson sentence, for example, English readers would more likely opt for *I and this woman were dwelling in one (the same) house*, over *I and this woman, dwellers in one house.* (Actually, English readers would probably change the word order to *This woman and I …*)

?   Render the roots below as Qal participles:

_____ **בוא** (f. sg.)   _____ **קום** (m. sg.)   _____ **הלך** (m. sg.)

_____ **אמר** (f. pl.)   _____ **נתן** (m. pl.)   _____ **סור** (f. sg.) [1]

?   Translate:

_____ מִלְחָמָה   _____ מִלְחֶמֶת־   _____ מִלְחַמְתָּהּ

_____ יָדָהּ   _____ הַבָּאָה   _____ יָרְדָה [2]

———

[1]   בוא ← בָּאָה (f. sg.)   קום ← קָם (m. sg.)   הלך ← הֹלֵךְ (m. sg.)

אמר ← אֹמְרוֹת (f. pl.)   נתן ← נֹתְנִים (m. pl.)   סור ← סָרָה (f. sg.)

[2] war מִלְחָמָה   war of מִלְחֶמֶת־   her war מִלְחַמְתָּהּ

her hand יָדָהּ   the one (f. sg.) who was coming הַבָּאָה   she descended יָרְדָה

62

◆

וְלֹא־נָתַן יְהוה לָכֶם לֵב לָדַעַת וְעֵינַֽיִם לִרְאוֹת וְאָזְנַֽיִם לִשְׁמֹעַ
עַד הַיּוֹם הַזֶּה:

Deuteronomy 29:3

S 25.7   Write the Qal infinitive construct for each of the following roots:

?	ילד _____	עבר _____	שׂים _____	ירד _____
	עשׂה _____	נתן _____	נפל _____	מות _____
	שׁמר _____	הלך _____	יצא _____	לקח ¹ _____

---

¹ ילד ← לֶדֶת   עבר ← עֲבֹר   שׂים ← שִׂים   ירד ← רֶדֶת

עשׂה ← עֲשׂוֹת   נתן ← תֵּת   נפל ← נְפֹל   מות ← מוֹת

שׁמר ← שְׁמֹר   הלך ← לֶכֶת   יצא ← צֵאת   לקח ← קַחַת

LESSON 26

וְאַתֶּם רְאִיתֶם אֵת כָּל־אֲשֶׁר עָשָׂה יהוה אֱלֹהֵיכֶם

Joshua 23:3

S 26.5a **What is the י all about in the affix of 3rd ה verbs?**

Most 3rd ה roots derive from original 3rd י roots.[1] That "original" י is manifested in the affix in those PGNs whose affix pronoun begins with a consonant, that is, the second and first persons:

2 m. sg.	בָּנִיתָ		2 m. pl.	בְּנִיתֶם
2 f. sg.	בָּנִית		2f. pl.	בְּנִיתֶן
1 c. sg.	בָּנִיתִי		1 c. pl.	בָּנִינוּ

The third person has a different response to this weakness.

?

3 m. sg. keeps the ה (because nothing follows it). Write: **he built** _____

3 f. sg. ה becomes ת[2] Write: **she built:** _____

3 c. pl. the ה elides. Write: **they built:** _____ **3**

To sum up: ה as a root letter in the third position of a verb does one of four things:

?

1) It remains _____

2) It becomes ת _____

3) It elides _____

---

[1] Some derive from original 3rd ו and a few are considered to be genuine 3rd ה These have a mappiq in the final ה showing that the ה is a genuine consonant.

[2] Final feminine הָ becomes ת in verbs and/or nouns when another element is added to the word. Here it is the affix pronoun.

[3] **he built** בָּנָה Note: This is a rare instance when the הָ endiNG is not 3 f. sg.

she built בָּנְתָה

they built בָּנוּ Note: וֹה at the end of the word is almost always the suffix "him."

64

4) It is represented as י _____ **4**

S 26.5b **How does the 3rd ה act in the Qal prefix?**

1) The ה is present in those PGNs that don't have a prefix complement.

?

Write: we will build _____ I will build _____

you (m. sg.)/she will build _____ he will build _____ **5**

2) The ה elides when the prefix complement is a vowel.

Write: you (m. pl.) will build _____ they (m. pl.) will build _____

you (f. sg.) will build _____ **6**

3) The ה is represented by the "original" י when the prefix complement begins with a consonant.

?

Write: you (f. pl.) and they (f. pl.) will build _____ _____ **7**

?

Translate: _____ בָּנָה _____ בָּנֶה _____ בָּנָה

_____ בְּנִי _____ בָּנוֹת _____ תִּבְנֶה _____ בָּנוּ

_____ בָּנוּ _____ בָּנִינוּ _____ בָּנִים **8**

---

4 1) It remains <u>only</u> if nothing follows it (as in the 3 m. sg. affix).

2) It becomes ת in the 3 f. sg.

3) It elides in the 3 m. pl.

4) it is represented as י in the second and first persons.

5 we will build נִבְנֶה   I will build אֶבְנֶה

you (m. sg.)/she will build תִּבְנֶה   he will build יִבְנֶה

6 you (m. pl.) will build תִּבְנוּ   they (m. pl.) will build יִבְנוּ

you (f. sg.) will build תִּבְנִי

7 you (f. pl.) and they (f. pl.) will build תִּבְנֶינָה and תִּבְנֶינָה

8 build (m. sg.) בְּנֵה   builder (m. sg.) בָּנֶה   builder (f. sg.) בֹּנָה

build (f. sg.) בְּנִי   builders (f. pl.) בָּנוֹת   you (m. sg.)/she will build תִּבְנֶה   they built בָּנוּ

build (m. pl.) בְּנוּ   we built בָּנִינוּ   builders (m.pl.) בָּנִים

—

One more thing: nouns ending in הֶ֖ such as בֹּנֶה | הֶ֖ → הֶ֖ in construct.

?   Write: he is a builder _____ the builder of Zion _____ **9**

---

9   he is a builder בֹּנֶה   the builder of Zion בֹּנֵה צִיּוֹן

LESSON 27

⸻

וְלֹא־שָׁבוּ אֶל־יְהוָה אֱלֹהֵיהֶם

Hosea 7:10

S 27.1   **Are 3rd ה and hollow roots often ambiguous?**

Two forms are: שָׁבָה and שָׁבוּ

?   Give two possibilities for both שָׁבָה and שָׁבוּ

_____ **1**

S 27.4a   **What are the peculiarities of hollow verbs in the Qal affix?**

In the Qal affix, the main types of hollow verbs exemplified in the verb charts by שִׂים קוֹם בּוֹא lose the middle letter and conjugate similarly.

?   Write:

he stood up_____   they came _____   she put _____ **2**

But in the second and first persons sg. and pl., the vowel under the first root letter is

_____ **3**

?   Write:

I put _____   you (m. sg.) stood up _____   you (m. pl.) put _____ **4**

T or F   Because בּוֹא ends in an א the qamats under the בּ remains throughout the affix conjugation.**5**

⸻

1 שָׁבָה could be the 3 m. sg. affix of שָׁבָה or the 3 f. sg. affix of שׁוּב

שָׁבוּ could be the 3 c. pl. of either שָׁבָה or שׁוּב

2 he stood up קָם   they came בָּאוּ   she put שָׂמָה

3 Patah ַ

4 I put שַׂמְתִּי   you (m. sg.) stood up קַמְתָּ   you (m. pl.) put שַׂמְתֶּם

5 True.

67

S 27.4b   **What are the characteristics of hollow verbs in the prefix form?**

In the prefix form, the hollow vowel stays, each according to its origin, and as in the vav conversive the vowel under the prefix pronoun is qamats ָ

?   Write:

we will stand up _____   she will come _____   I will put _____ **6**

?   In the prefix form with vav conversive, the hollow vowel may be shortened. Write the prefix forms without vav conversive for the verbs below:

7 וַיָּ֫מָת _____   וַיָּ֫שֶׂם _____   וַיָּ֫קָם _____   וַיָּקֻ֫מוּ _____

S 27.4c   **Is there anything unusual about hollow verbs in the imperative?**

?   The imperatives are formed like other imperatives:_____ **8**

?   Analyze:

9 שִׂ֫ימוּ _____   בּ֫וֹאִי _____   קֹ֫מְנָה _____

S 27.4d   **Is there anything unusual about Qal participles of hollow verbs?**

_____ **10**

?   Write: And behold! Rachel was coming with the sheep that were her father's.

_____ **11**

---

6   we will stand up נָק֫וּם   she will come תָּבוֹא   I will put אָשִׂים

7 וַיָּ֫מָת ← יָמוּת   וַיָּ֫שֶׂם ← יָשִׂים   וַיָּ֫קָם ← יָקוּם   וַיָּקֻ֫מוּ ← יָק֫וּמוּ

8 The imperative is formed by removing the prefix pronoun from the prefix form.

9 בּ֫וֹאִי is the f. sg. imperative of בּוֹא   שִׂ֫ימוּ is the pl. imperative of שִׂים
קֹ֫מְנָה is the f. pl. imperative of קוּם

10 They do not have ḥolem after the first root letter. They have qamats. See 9.5a and 24.5b.

11 וְהִנֵּה רָחֵל בָּאָה עִם הַצֹּאן אֲשֶׁר לְאָבִיהָ

אֱלֹהֵיהֶם

וְלֹא־שָׁבוּ אֶל־יהוה אֱלֹהֵיהֶם

T or F In BDB all verbs are listed under the 3 m. sg. Qal affix form.¹²

? Write the infinitive construct for:

turn aside _____ die _____ enter _____ return _____ **13**

? Translate the following verbs:

you (m. pl.) turned aside_____ we died _____ arise (f. sg.) _____

you (m. pl.) will return _____ they arose _____ she returned _____

I will put _____ he turned aside _____ you (f. pl.) will enter _____ **14**

---

¹² False. For hollows, BDB uses the infinitive to get three root letters.

¹³turn aside **סוּר** die **מוּת** enter **בּוֹא** return **שׁוּב**

¹⁴ you (m. pl.) turned aside **סַרְתֶּם** we died **מַתְנוּ** arise (f. sg.) **קוּמִי**

you (m. pl.) will return **תָּשׁוּבוּ** they arose **קָמוּ** she returned **שָׁבָה**

I will put **אָשִׂים** he turned aside **סָר** you (f. pl.) will enter **תָּבֹאנָה**

69

LESSON 28

וְהַמֶּ֣לֶךְ אָסָ֗א הִשְׁמִ֙יעַ֙ אֶת־כָּל־יְהוּדָ֔ה

1 Kings 15:22

S 28.5   **Why, in the Hif`il affix, does only the third person have hireq between the second and third root letters?**

Practical answer: Affix pronouns that are consonants often affect the vowel in the syllable before them. We have seen this in hollows and 3rd ה verbs. Here we can see that even a stem preformative can stimulate such a change. For a complex (and, be cautioned, hypothetical) answer, see Gesenius §53*a* or Joüon §54*a*.[1]

?   Write the Hif`il affix of קרב in the following PGNs:

3 f. sg. _____   1 c. sg. _____   1 c. pl. _____

3 m. pl _____   2 f. pl _____   3 m. sg _____ [2]

?   **Weak Verb Review**

In which forms do 1st י verbs of the ידד type lose the י of the root?

_____

In which forms do 1st י verbs of the ירד type _not_ lose the י of the root?

_____

---

[1] At one point in the discussion, Joüon appeals to Philippi's law, which states that in a closed, stressed syllable, I → A (hireq → patah). That seems to be reason enough for the patah in the second person sg. and the first person sg. and pl., but not the second person pl., in which the final syllable gets the stress.

[2] 3 f. sg.   הִקְרִיבָה   1 c. sg.   הִקְרַבְתִּי   1 c. pl.   הִקְרַבְנוּ

3 m. pl.   הִקְרִיבוּ   2 f. pl.   הִקְרַבְתֶּן   3 m. sg.   הִקְרִיב

70

In the Qal affix of hollows, what is peculiar about the initial vowel in the second and first persons?

_____

In 3rd ה verbs, in the affix, what happens to the ה in the second and first person?

_____

In 3rd ה verbs, in the affix, what happens to the ה in the 3 f. sg.?

_____

In 3rd ה verbs, in the affix, what happens to the ה in the 3 c. pl.?

_____

In 3rd ה verbs, in the prefix form, when is there a י after the first two root letters?

_____

(For answers to questions above, see Verb Charts D, H, and I.)

שׁבה	שׁוב	ישׁב
capture	*return*	*dwell*

?   Translate:

C	B	A
שָׁבָה _____	_____ שָׁב	יָשַׁב _____ 1
יָשַׁבְתִּי _____	_____ שַׁבְתִּי	שָׁבִיתִי _____ 2
_____ שָׁבוּ	שְׁבִיתֶם _____	יָשְׁבָה _____ 3
_____ שְׁבָה	_____ שֵׁב	שׁוּבִי _____ 4
שְׁבִי _____	_____ שֵׁבוּ	שְׁבוּ _____ 5
תִּשְׁבֶּה _____	_____ תָּשׁוּב	תֵּשֵׁב _____ 6
שֹׁבוֹת _____	_____ יוֹשְׁבוֹת	שֹׁבוֹת _____ 7
_____ שֶׁבְנָה	שֹׁבְנָה _____	שְׁבֶינָה _____ 8
יָשַׁבְנוּ _____	_____ שָׁבִינוּ	שַׁבְנוּ _____ 9
_____ שְׁבוֹת	_____ שֶׁבֶת	לָשׁוּב 10³

3

C	B	A
1 he captured/she returned *or* returning one (f. sg.)	he returned *or* returning one (m. sg.)	he dwelled
2 I dwelled	I returned	I captured
3 they returned/captured	you captured (m. pl.)	she dwelled
4 capture! (m. sg.)	dwell! (m. sg.)	return (f. sg.) /my returning
5 dwell/capture! (f. sg.)	return! (m. pl.)	dwell/capture! (m. pl.)
6 she/you (m. sg.) will capture	she/you (m. sg.) will return	she/you (m. sg.) will dwell
7 returning (f. pl.)	dwellers (f. pl.)	capturing (f. pl.)
8 dwell! (f. pl.)	return! (f. pl.)	capture! (f. pl.)
9 we dwelled	we captured	we returned
10 to capture	to dwell	to return

72

LESSON 29

וְהָיָה אֱלֹהִים עִמָּכֶם וְהֵשִׁיב אֶתְכֶם אֶל־אֶרֶץ אֲבֹתֵיכֶם

Genesis 48:21

S 29.1   **Why is there a dagesh in the מ of עִמָּכֶם**

The root of the preposition עַם is עִמַּם but the gemination will show only when there is a suffix because final geminated letters are rarely written.

S 29.3   **Do all nouns using ות__ for their plurals have an extra י before a suffix?**

Not all, but most. One suffix that does not always demand the extra י is the 3 m. pl. One could see either תּוֹרוֹתָם or תּוֹרוֹתֵיהֶם both meaning *their Torahs*.

S 29.5   **In the Hif'il affix of hollow verbs, why is the preformative of the third persons pointed הֵ __**

There may not be a completely satisfactory answer. (See Joüon § 80*g* or Gesenius § 72*w*). It is more likely phonetic than grammatical.

?   Write: he caused-to-return _____ they caused-to-enter _____ [1]

S 29.5.1   **In the second and first persons, why is the Hif'il preformative pointed הֲ and why is there a ḥolem before the affix pronoun?**

The initial reduced vowel is due to the first syllable's distance from the accent (as in the Qal affix of the same persons). Here the shewa is composite because it is under a guttural הֲ The ḥolem וֹ a "separating" or "linking" vowel in the second and first persons, usually though not always present, does not yield a simple explanation (see Gesenius §72 *i* or Joüon §80 *i*). Its purpose is to keep the middle syllable open. (However, why that is necessary is not clear.)

---

1   He caused-to-return הֵשִׁיב   they caused-to-enter הֵבִיאוּ

73

וְהָיָה אֱלֹהִים עִמָּכֶם וְהֵשִׁיב אֶתְכֶם אֶל־אֶרֶץ אֲבֹתֵיכֶם

Common hollows found in the Hif`il are:

בּוֹא שׁוּב מוּת קוּם נוּחַ רוּם סוּר

? Write:

they killed _____

you (m. pl.) established _____

he brought back _____

we exalted _____

you (m. sg.) brought in _____

you (m. pl.) removed _____

I established _____ **2**

? Translate:

B		A	
תּוֹרֹתֵּינוּ _____		עֵדֹתְכֶם _____	1
רָבוּ _____		בַּקֵּשׁ _____	2
מַעֲשֵׂה־יָדֶיךָ _____		תִּירְשׁוּ _____	3
שָׁתִיתִי _____		הִקְרַבְתֶּן _____	4
אֱסוֹר _____		אֹיְבֵיהֶם _____	5
וְנָתַנּוּ _____		הֲיְדַעְתֶּם _____	6
אֹתוֹ _____		זְכֹר _____	7
עֵת לָלֶדֶת _____		וּבְכֹתָהּ _____	8
הִגְדַּלְתְּ _____		נְשֵׁי־שְׁלֹמֹה _____	9
שָׂנְאוּ _____		בְּנוֹתַי _____	10
קָמִים _____		לָתֵת לָכֶם _____	11
הֵשִׁיב _____		לֹא־כֵן הָרְשָׁעִים _____	12
תִּשֹׁבְנָה _____		וְשַׁבְתִּי _____	13

---

2 they killed הֵמִיתוּ

you (m. pl.) established הֲקִימוֹתֶם

he brought back הֵשִׁיב

we exalted הֲרִימוֹנוּ

you (m. sg.) brought in הֵבֵאתָ

you (m. pl.) removed הֲסִירוֹתֶם

I established הֲקִימוֹתִי

וְהָיָה אֱלֹהִים עִמָּכֶם וְהֵשִׁיב אֶתְכֶם אֶל־אֶרֶץ אֲבֹתֵיכֶם

_____ גָּלִינוּ		_____ רֵד מֹשֶׁה	14
_____ מָלְאָה		_____ בְּקִרְבּוֹ	15
_____ לַיְלָה טוֹב		_____ אַל־תִּירְאִי	16
_____ חָטָאתָ		_____ אָהֵב	17
_____ אֵשֶׁת־חַיִל		_____ הָיְתָה[3]	18

3

	B		A
1	our Torot (teachings)		your (pl.) testimony (sg.)
2	they became many		seek! (m. sg. Pi`el)
3	the work of your hands		you (m. pl.) will inherit
4	I drank		you (f. pl.) caused to draw near
5	I will turn aside		their (m.) enemies (m.)
6	and we will give		Do/did you (m. pl.) know?
7	him (DDO)		remember (m. sg. imperative or infinitive)
8	a time to bear		and she will weep
9	you (f. sg.) caused to become great		the wives of Solomon
10	Hate! (m. pl. imp.)		my daughters
11	(the ones) arising (m.)		to give to you (m. pl.)
12	he caused to return		not so the wicked (Ps. 1)
13	they/you (f. pl.) will return		and I will return
14	we uncovered		go down (m. sg. imperative) Moses (vocative)
15	she was full		in his midst
16	good night		do not fear (f. sg.)
17	you (m. sg.) sinned		he loved (Qal affix, 3 m. sg. I class verb)
18	a woman of substance (Prov. 31)		she became

LESSON 30

הַגִּידָה לִּי מֶה עָשִׂיתָה

1 Samuel 14:43

S 30.1   **What distinguishes הַגִּידָה from a f. noun with the definite article?**

It's subtle. A feminine noun would be accented on the last syllable. The form הַגִּידָה is confusing because of the extra final ה ָ an addition one may see on m. sg. imperatives. Some grammarians attribute this additional ה ָ to analogy with the cohortative as in וַאֲנִי וְהַנַּעַר נֵלְכָה עַד־כֹּה which you saw in Genesis 22:5 and which will be studied formally in Lesson 41. In any event, do not mix up the lengthened m. sg. imperative הַגִּידָה with the f. sg. imperative, which has a prefix complement: הַגִּידִי

S 30.3   **In the lesson sentence, why is מֶה spelled מֶה**

מֶה מָה מַה are all vocalizations of *what*. Although מַה tends to be used most often before maqqef, and מֶה before ע there does not seem to be a strict relationship between the vocalization of "what" with what follows. Distance from the accent may be influential. There is a phenomenon called "differentiation" (so Joüon, § 29*h*; called "dissimilation" by Gesenius, § 27*w*), which Joüon notes is "a tendency to avoid a sequence of two vowels of identical or similar timbre." Gesenius and Joüon are speaking about this within a word, but it may happen between words, too. On the other hand, there is a phenomenon of "mirroring," in which the tendency is just the opposite: a vowel is chosen because it sounds like another. In mirroring, however, a composite shewa influences a preceding vocal shewa to become the full vowel of its half vowel: וְעֶשֵׂה ← וַעֲשֵׂה

S 30.3.1   **Would you explain again why עָשִׂיתָה has ה at the end?**

It is a plene spelling.[1] Sometimes ה at the end of a word "holds" an A sound. It happens most often in the 2 m. sg. affix of 3rd ה verbs. (This ה ָ is not analogous to the ending of the imperative הַגִּידָה where a syllable is actually added.)

---

[1] Sometimes a final ה is deleted giving a defectiva spelling, as when a plural prefix form ending in נָה ‿ for example, is written ן ‿

76

LESSON 31

◀━━▶

הֵם הַמְדַבְּרִים אֶל־פַּרְעֹה מֶלֶךְ־מִצְרַיִם לְהוֹצִיא אֶת־בְּנֵי־יִשְׂרָאֵל מִמִּצְרָיִם

Exodus 6:27

S 31.1   **The Piʿel prefix is יְדַבֵּר etc.; the participle is מְדַבֵּר Is this a pattern?**

Yes. Remove the prefix pronoun or preformative מ and the imperative and infinitive emerge.

?   Write the Piʿel imperatives of דבר

m. sg. _____   m. pl. _____   f. sg. _____   f. pl. _____¹

S 31.2   **Is הו⌐ reserved for Hifʿils of 1st י verbs or could it indicate a Qal participle?**

הו⌐ could certainly start a Qal participle of a first ה verb, for example, הוֹרֵג and הוֹלֵךְ In the case of הוֹצִיא the root הצא is not extant, so the ה must be a preformative. Also, the Qal participle does not have ḥireq ⌐ in the medial position.

Note: Many 1st י verbs that are "strong" in the Qal, in that they keep the י of the root in the prefix form, do not maintain that strength in the derived stems; in those the י reverts to this older ו So one sees יִירַשׁ *he will inherit*, but הוֹרִישׁ *he has caused to inherit*.

?   Translate:

הֹלְכוֹת _____   הוֹצֵאת _____   לְהוֹלִיד _____²

---

¹ m. sg. דַּבֵּר   m. pl. דַּבְּרוּ   f. sg. דַּבְּרִי   f. pl. דַּבֵּרְנָה

² הֹלְכוֹת going (f. pl.)   הוֹצֵאת you (f. sg.) brought out   לְהוֹלִיד to beget

77

LESSON 32

וַיָּגֵד מֹשֶׁה אֶת־דִּבְרֵי הָעָם אֶל־יהוה

Exodus 19:9

S 32.1   **Is וַיָּגֵד related (other than by root) to הִגִּידָה (Lesson 30)? Both have pataḥ under a preformative element.**

Yes. Pataḥ ◌ַ under the preformative element is a sign of the Hif`il of the strong verb (and some weak verbs) in all forms except the affix. Note also that both words have an I class vowel ◌ֵ ◌ִ ◌ֵ between the second and third root letters, also a fairly consistent feature of the stem.

S 32.3a   **Do all vav conversives shorten the same way?**

First, to be clear, not all vav conversives shorten.[1] Qals of weak verbs and Hif`ils of both strong and weak verbs do; strong verbs tend not to. When shortening does occur, it is of two kinds:

1)   A long (or longer) second vowel in the prefix form (**without** vav conversive) reconverts to a short (or shorter) one in the prefix form **with** vav conversive. But the vowel does not change class. In other words:

tsere ◌ֵ or ḥireq ◌ִ may go to segol ◌ֶ   יָשִׂים → וַיָּשֶׂם

ḥolem וֹ or shureq וּ may go to qamats ḥatuf ◌ָ   יָקוּם → וַיָּקָם

shureq וּ may go to qibbuts ◌ֻ   יָקוּמוּ → וַיָּקֻמוּ   and so on

2)   The other kind occurs with 3rd ה verbs. The ◌ֶה ending of the prefix form apocopates (falls off the end), and there may be a vowel change under the prefix pronoun. Examples:[2] יִרְאֶה →וַיַּרְא   יִהְיֶה →וַיְהִי

---

[1] It may be that the prefix form and the prefix form with vav conversive are historically different entities. See chapters 31 and 33 in Waltke and O'Connor for a discussion of theories about their possible origins.

[2] If you want to read about these vowel changes, see Gesenius § 75 *o–t*.

? Write the following as prefix forms without vav conversive:

_____ וַיִּבֶן	_____ וַיִּבֶן	_____ וַיָּקֻמוּ
_____ וַתָּמָת	_____ וַיַּרְא	_____ וַתֵּשֶׁב
_____ וַתֵּלְכִי	_____ וַיִּפֹּל	_____ [3] וַיּוֹלֶד

---

[3] וַיִּבֶן ← יִבְנֶה	וַיִּבֶן ← יָבִין	וַיָּקֻמוּ ← יָקוּמוּ
וַתָּמָת ← נָמוּת	וַיַּרְא ← יִרְאֶה	וַתֵּשֶׁב ← תֵּשֵׁב
וַתֵּלְכִי ← תֵּלְכִי	וַיִּפֹּל ← יִפֹּל	וַיּוֹלֶד ← יוֹלִיד

LESSON 33

◆

וָאוֹצִיא אֶת־אֲבוֹתֵיכֶם מִמִּצְרַיִם

Joshua 24:6

S 33.1   Again, is it possible to think "Qal participle" for a word such as וָאוֹצִיא

As with הו ‿ there may be a temptation when seeing או ‿ to go that route (imagin-ing the root in this case to be אצא), but two particular features of the word militate against that possibility. One is the medial vowel ḥireq ‿ִי (see **S 31.2**); the other is that וָא announces vav conversive for the 1 c. sg. prefix pronoun, since the syllable וָ not being pretonic, does not represent lengthening (the qamets ‿ָ is compensating for the dagesh, which would be in the prefix pronoun were it not a guttural. See **S 11.2**).

S 33.5   Analyze the following Hifʿils:

?	B		A	
	הוֹדִעֵנִי _____		תַּפְקִיד _____	1
	מוֹלֶדֶת _____		הִפִּילוּ _____	2
	הִגְדַּלְתָּ _____		הוֹשַׁע _____	3
	מַחֲזִיקִים _____		יַעֲבִירוּ _____	4
	הֵכִין _____		הֲסִירוֹתִי _____	5¹

	B		**A**	
1	m. sg. Hifʿil imperative + 1 c. sg. suffix	ידע	3 f./2 m. sg. Hifʿil prefix	פקד
2	f. sg. Hifʿil participle	ילד	3 c. pl. Hifʿil affix	נפל
3	2 m. sg. Hifʿil affix	גדל	3 m. sg. Hifʿil aff./imp./infin.	ישע
4	m. pl. Hifʿil participle	חזק	3 m. pl. Hifʿil prefix	עבר
5	3 m. sg. Hifʿil affix	כון	1 c. sg. Hifʿil affix	סור

LESSON 34

וַיַּכּוּ אֶת־גְּדַלְיָהוּ בֶן־אֲחִיקָם בֶּן־שָׁפָן בַּחֶרֶב וַיָּמֶת אֹתוֹ

Jeremiah 41:2

S 34.1   **Identify the verbs below as Qal or Hif`il**

?   יִשְׁטֶה וַיֵּט יֵט יִשְׁטֶה וַתֵּט וְאָט יֵט וַתֵּט הִשָּׂא וַיִּטּוּ נָטָה [1]

S 34.1.1   **Which take precedence, features of the stem or demands of the root?**

<u>Significant point</u>: In 3rd ה the features of that end of the verb take precedence over stem characteristics, no matter what the stem. (Since stem influence is from the front to the middle of a word, that makes sense.) Note that in hollows the features of the stem take precedence over the hollow vowel, as הָקִים   and   יָקִים   (Hif`ils of קוּם) illustrate. (Review 29.5.)

S 34.6   **Are I class hollows common?**

No, quite rare. Lesson 17 showed that the Qal affix can have an I or U class vowel in the second position כָּבֵד   or   קָטֹן   for example, instead of the more usual A class vowel as in פָּקַד   Hollows are not immune from that phenomenon. There is one common I class hollow (so called because like כָּבֵד it takes tsere ֵ under the first root letter in the 3 m. sg. affix form): מוּת and there are two common U class hollows: טוֹב *be good* and   בּוֹשׁ *be ashamed*. Their class vowel shows in the same PGNs as in the strong verb.

?   Write:

we died _____   she died _____   they died _____   you (m. sg.) died _____ [2]

?   What does the dagesh in מַתִּי מֵתָה מֵת etc. represent? _____ [3]

---

[1] Q נָטָה Q וַיִּטּוּ Hi. הִשָּׂא Q וַתֵּט Q וְאָט Hi. יֵט Q יֵט Q יִשְׁטֶה Q וַתֵּט Hi. וַיֵּט Hi. יִשְׁטֶה

[2]   we died מַתְנוּ   she died מֵתָה   they died מֵתוּ   you (m. sg.) died מַתָּה

[3] It represents the root letter ת   Affix and prefix pronouns do not assimilate.

S 34.6.1 Does the I class vowel carry over into the prefix or any other forms of מוּת

No. In the other forms מוּת acts like a regular hollow.

? Write:

he will die _____   you (m. sg.) will die _____   you (m. pl.) will die _____ **4**

S 34.6.2 Does the "participle" of מוּת decline like the participles of other hollow verbs?

Yes, even with the same ambiguity מֵת he died/he is dead

?

_____ she died/she is dead

_____ they (m.) are dead **5**

S 34.6.3 How does the affix form of the U class hollow בּוֹשׁ conjugate?

Qal Affix בּוֹשׁ

sg.	3 m.	בֹּשׁ	pl.	3 c.	בֹּשׁוּ
	3 f.	בּוֹשָׁה			
	2 m.	בֹּשְׁתָּ		2 m.	בָּשְׁתֶּם
	2 f.	בֹּשְׁתְּ		2 f.	בָּשְׁתֶּן
	1 c.	בֹּשְׁתִּי		1 c.	בֹּשְׁנוּ

Note that the U class vowel persists throughout the conjugation (compare with קָטֹן)
(17.6c). In the 2 m/f. pl., that vowel is represented by _____ **6**

S 34.6.4 In the **Qal prefix**, בּוֹשׁ has ◌ָ under the prefix pronoun יֵבוֹשׁ

? The usual vowel under the prefix pronoun for a hollow in the Qal is _____ **7**

S 34.6.5 The only extant **Qal participle** is בּוֹשִׁים *they are ashamed.*

---

[4] he will die יָמוּת   you (m. sg.) will die תָּמוּת   you (m. pl.) will die תָּמוּתוּ

[5]   she died/is dead מֵתָה   they are dead מֵתִים

[6] Qamats ḥatuf

[7] Qamats

?	The usual first vowel for a hollow in the Qal participle is _____ [8]
§ 34.6.6	The imperative and infinitive are "normal."
?	Write the infinitive of בּוּשׁ _____ f. sg. and m. pl. imperatives _____ [9]

---

[8] Qamats

[9] infinitive בּוּשׁ   f. sg. imperative בּוּשִׁי   m. pl. imperative בּוּשׁוּ

LESSON 35

◆

בִּהְיוֹת שָׁאוּל מֶלֶךְ אַתָּה הַמּוֹצִיא וְהַמֵּבִיא אֶת־יִשְׂרָאֵל

1 Chronicles 11:2

S 35.6.4   **Can a suffix on an infinitive ever be the object of the infinitive?**

It can be the object although that is far less usual. In Genesis 37:4 there is such an example:

וְלֹא יָכְלוּ דַּבְּרוֹ לְשָׁלֹם

and they were not able to speak <u>to him</u> with shalom

?   Translate:

_____ בְּמָלְכוֹ

_____ כִּשְׁמֹעַ לָבָן

_____ אַחֲרֵי רְאוֹתִי אֶת־פָּנֶיךָ

_____ בְּהַרְאֹתוֹ

_____ וּבְלֶכְתְּךָ [1]

?   What is the preformative (with vowel) of the Hif‘il participle of each of the following?

strong verb _____   hollow _____   1st י _____ [2]

---

[1]

when he was king	בְּמָלְכוֹ
when Laban heard	כִּשְׁמֹעַ לָבָן
after I saw your face	אַחֲרֵי רְאוֹתִי אֶת־פָּנֶיךָ
when he showed	בְּהַרְאֹתוֹ
and when you walk	וּבְלֶכְתְּךָ

[2]   strong verb מַ ‍ַ   hollow מֵ ‍ֵ   1st י מוֹ

84

LESSON 36

כִּי־אַתָּה תְּבָרֵךְ צַדִּיק יהוה

Psalms 5:13

S 36.3   **What are the perils of the Pi'el?**

Any situation that would cause the dagesh in the middle root letter not to show is a problem.

1) Mid-gutturals are one category, and most disconcerting is that not all mid-gutturals react the same way. ר ע א are most likely to require compensatory lengthening, ה ח least likely. So, knowing the two major vowel patterns: affix and prefix is important!

?   he spoke is דִּבֶּר   he blessed _____

   he will speak _____   he will bless _____ **1**

?   Write the Pi'els of בְרֵךְ in the following forms:

   m. sg. participle _____   1 c. pl. prefix _____   m. pl. imperative _____

   2 f. pl. affix _____   m. pl. participle _____   3f. pl. prefix _____ **2**

2) When the middle root letter is the last letter of the word, as would be the case in the vav conversive of a 3rd ה for example, the dagesh won't show וַיְצַו *and he commanded.*

3) And, of course, shewa can make dagesh forte disappear, as in the prefix pronoun of וַיְצַו

---

1   he spoke דִּבֶּר   he blessed בֵּרֵךְ

   he will speak יְדַבֵּר   he will bless יְבָרֵךְ

2   m. sg. participle מְבָרֵךְ   1 c. pl. prefix נְבָרֵךְ   m. pl. imperative בָּרְכוּ

   2 f. pl. affix בֵּרַכְתֶּן   m. pl. participle מְבָרְכִים   3 f. pl. prefix תְּבָרֵכְנָה

85

S 36.3b   **Is it correct to think that shewa can make dagesh forte disappear in any situation in which a letter requires a dagesh forte?**

Yes. Whether that letter is the middle root letter of a Pi'el, definite article, assimilated letter, etc.

S 36.4   **What is the function of the dagesh in צַדִּיק**

It is simply an intrinsic part of its formation. Joüon would classify it as a "qattil" (§88 I *c*). Lambdin (§50) calls it a noun with two unchangeable syllables.

S 36.7   **Verbs are conjugated in the order of third-second-first persons. Why are independent subject pronouns listed in the chart in the order first-second-third?**

It is simply a common organizational convention. The reason for the third-second-first organization for verbs is that the names of the stems, based on the paradigmatic פָּעַל are modeled on the 3 m. sg. affix pattern:

$$\text{פָּעַל} \longrightarrow \text{פָּקַד}$$
$$\text{הִפְעִיל} \longrightarrow \text{הִפְקִיד}$$
$$\text{נִפְעַל} \longrightarrow \text{נִפְקַד}$$

S 36.7.1   **Are the independent subject pronouns arbitrary words or do they have a connection to affix, prefix, and/or object pronouns of the corresponding PGN?**

אֲנִי   "I" has its second syllable echoed in the suffixes יִ◌ and נִי◌ *my/me*.

אַתָּה   "You" m. sg. finds its second syllable in the 2 m. sg. affix pronoun תָ◌ sometimes spelled תָה◌ as in עָשִׂיתָה (30.3). Conversely, the independent אַתְּ without ה occurs five times (but is to be read as if אַתָּה). Note: The dagesh in the ת represents an assimilated נ אַנְתָּה←אַתָּה

אַתְּ   "You" f. sg. sees its second letter in the 2 f. sg. affix pronoun פָּקַדְתְּ But אַתְּ was, earlier, אַתִּי (it appears that way five times in the Biblical text) and before that, אַנְתִּי MT still preserves the תִי◌ affix pronoun when a suffix is added, thus making the 2 f. sg. affix + suffix (rather rare) identical to the 1 c. sg. affix + suffix. Common sense will have to rule when one encounters one of these combinations.

Also, the vestigial י appears in the 2 f. sg. prefix form תִּשְׁמְרִי *she will keep* and consequently in the imperative שִׁמְרִי *keep*, for example.

הוּא   "He" or "that one" appears without the א as הוּ◌ the 3 m. sg. attached object suffix, as in וְהַעֲלֵהוּ *and offer him up* (Gen. 22:2).

הִיא   "She" sees its הַ in the object suffix written הָ‎ or ֶה   <u>Note</u>: הִיא is regularly written הוא in MT. This is an example of *qere perpetuum*.[3]

אֲנַחְנוּ   "We." Its final syllable נוּ‎ is seen both as an affix pronoun: פְּקַדְנוּ *we visited* and as a possessive or object suffix "our" or "us:" אָחִינוּ *our brother*, לָנוּ *to us*. Occasionally in Biblical Hebrew אֲנַחְנוּ is expressed as נַחְנוּ or the even shorter אָנוּ (written this way in Mishnaic Hebrew).

אַתֶּם   "You." m. pl. Its second syllable is seen as the 2 m. pl. affix pronoun תֶּם‎

אַתֵּן אַתֵּנָה   "You" f. pl. Its second syllable is also apparent in the corresponding 2 f. pl. affix pronoun תֶּן‎

הֵם הֵמָּה   "They" m. is reflected in the 3 m. pl. possessive and object suffix הֶם‎ written ֶם‎ when it follows a consonant.

הֵן הֵנָּה   "They" f. is reflected in the possessive and object suffix הֶן‎ or ֶן‎

The 3. m. sg. הוא and 3. f. sg. הִיא and their plural counterparts, הֶם and הֶן respectively, are of special interest because they also function as the far attributive adjectives: "that" and "those."[4] When performing that function, they act like any other attributive adjective, following the noun and agreeing in gender, number, and definiteness. Granted these demonstratives are by definition definite, but nevertheless they take the added definite article when functioning attributively:

הָאָרֶץ הַהִיא *that land*   הָאֲנָשִׁים הָהֵם *those men*

Without the definite article, they function as predicate demonstratives:

הוּא הָאִישׁ *that is the man* or *he is the man*

---

[3] *Qere perpetuum* means "perpetual reading." In the case of some words, the form traditionally read is always different from that suggested by the letters. For more detail, see Yeivin, §106, *Introduction to the Tiberian Masorah*. Other examples of *qere perpetuum* are the tetragrammaton יְהֹוָה which is read אֲדֹנָי and יְרוּשָׁלַםִ which is regularly written without the י‎

[4] The close attributive adjectives are זֶה *this* (m. sg.) זֹאת *this* (f. sg.) אֵלֶּה *these* (c. pl.)

LESSON 37

———◆———

מֵאֵת יהוה הָיְתָה זֹּאת

Psalms 118:23

S 37.1   **Are compound prepositions common in Hebrew?**

Yes. מִן אֶל לְ are the most common prepositions to combine with other prepositions (see Gesenius §119 *b–e*). מֵאֵת is a parade example.

In BDB, prepositions have a separate section toward the end of their listing for compounds. See, for example, מִן **9** or אֵת **4**. In the case of לְ the compounds are so many that they are subcategorized by function. For ease in searching, one might want to first look under the less common (or if a triple compound, the least common) word in the compound. For example, מִלִּפְנֵי is more easily located under פְּנֵי than under מִן

S 37.2   **Is this a good time to review 3rd ה verbs?**

Couldn't be better.

Diagnostic question: Regarding הָיְתָה What is the function of the ה (See **S 26.5a**, note2.)

?   Write:

we were _____	they built _____
he saw _____	I will build _____
you (f. pl.) will do _____	do! (f. sg.) _____
and you (f. pl) went up _____	they stretched out _____ [1]

---

[1]

we were	הָיִינוּ	they built	בָּנוּ
he saw	רָאָה	I will build	אֶבְנֶה
you (f. pl.) will do	תַּעֲשֶׂינָה	do! (f. sg.)	עֲשִׂי
and you (f. pl) went up	וַתַּעֲלֶן	they stretched out	נָטוּ

LESSON 38

וַיִּקָּחֵהוּ שָׁאוּל בַּיּוֹם הַהוּא וְלֹא נְתָנוֹ לָשׁוּב בֵּית אָבִיו:

1 Samuel 18:2

S 38.1 **When a word ends in וֹה‗ is the ה ever part of the root?**

Only when the word is a genuine 3rd ה denoted by its root having a mappiq in the ה
Otherwise in a word ending וֹה‗ the וֹה‗ will be the suffix *him.*

§ 38.1.1 **What are some of these genuine 3rd ה roots and how do they look?**

Genuine 3rd ה s are rare:

אֱלֹהַּ *God*   גָּבַהּ *be high*   הָמַהּ *hesitate*   נָגַהּ *shine*   תָּמַהּ *be surprised*

Among these, the word we have had the most experience with is אֱלֹהַּ which yields
אֱלֹהִים Its ה stays no matter what is added: אֱלֹהֵיהֶם אֱלֹהָיו and so on. To give an
example of a verb, we can use גָּבַהּ Its 3 c. sg. Qal affix is גָּבְהוּ (The mappiq shows only
when the ה is the last letter as in the 3 m. sg. affix.)

S 38.2a **Is בּ the only preposition that causes elision of the definite article?**

No. לּ and כּ also tend to cause elision of the definite article, for example:

לְהַיּוֹם←לַיּוֹם

S 38.3 **Is there a morphological distinction between a 3 m. sg. Qal affix+suffix and a**
m. sg. imperative+suffix?

Yes. But first a word about the potential confusion: both could have shewa under the first
root letter, the imperative because it is an intrinsic feature of the form: שְׁמַע *hear* and
שְׁמָעֵנִי *hear me,* and the affix + suffix due to propretonic reduction: נָתַן *he gave* (no confusion) but נְתָנוֹ *he gave him* (potential confusion).

Why the propretonic reduction?

A verb with a suffix acts like a noun with regard to shortening and lengthening of syllables. It tends to work like this: Pretonic lengthening and propretonic reduction. To review: The vowel just before the accent (or tone) will be lengthened if possible and the
vowel two places before the accent will be shortened. In נְתָנוֹ the accented syllable is the
final וֹנ‗ The syllable before it (pretonic) is lengthened from the pataḥ as in נָתַן to qa-

mats, and the syllable before that (propretonic) is reduced from qamats to shewa. That ex-plains נְתָנוֹ But there is an additional feature that distinguishes a 3 m. sg. affix + suffix from m. sg. imperative + suffix, and that is the vowel before the suffix. In the affix, it will be an A class vowel; in the imperative, an I class vowel.

?   Translate:

שָׁלֵחֵנִי _____	שָׁלַח _____	שָׁלַח _____
שְׁלָחֵנִי _____	שְׁלָחָנוּ _____	שָׁלַחְנוּ _____ 1

S 38.4   **Why is the vowel under the ל of לָשׁוּב qamats and not shewa?**

The explanation just above—pretonic lengthening—can hold here, but since one could argue that שׁוּב is not really a noun (although infinitives can function as nouns) one can appeal to another convention: When an element whose normal vowel is shewa (לְ for example) is prefixed to a word that is monosyllabic (שׁוּב for example), the shewa often is lengthened to qamats, as in לָשׁוּב Of course, that is just another way of defining pre-tonic lengthening!

S 38.5   **Review:** What is the function of the י in אָבִיו (S 10.2b)

?   Write:

his brother _____ the fathers _____ 2

S 38.7a   **Are suffixes on verbs different from suffixes on nouns?**

Most are the same, but נִי _me_ will not appear on a noun, and הוּ _him_ only rarely appears on plural nouns (and would then, of course, be translated _his_) and never on sin-gular nouns.

S 38.7b   **Can the vowel changes in examples 1–4 be explained?**

Yes, to an extent.

1)   שָׁמַר _he guarded_ but with a suffix: שְׁמָרָהּ _he guarded her._ שָׁ is reduced to שְׁ be-cause of propretonic reduction.

---

1 send me	שָׁלֵחֵנִי	send	שָׁלַח	he sent	שָׁלַח
he sent me	שְׁלָחֵנִי	he sent us	שְׁלָחָנוּ	we sent	שָׁלַחְנוּ
2		his brother	אָחִיו	the fathers	הָאָבוֹת

90

וַיִּקָּחֵהוּ שָׁאוּל בַּיּוֹם הַהוּא וְלֹא נְתָנוֹ לָשׁוּב בֵּית אָבִיו:

———

2) שָׁמַרְתָּ but with a suffix: שְׁמַרְתַּנִי | שָׁ is reduced to שְׁ because of propretonic reduction. The reason for the change of vowel under the affix pronoun is not so clear, but the class of vowel has not changed: ַ and ֡ are both A class vowels.

3) יִשְׁמֹר but with a suffix: יִשְׁמְרֵנִי   In the prefix and imperative, when there is no prefix complement and a suffix is added, an I class vowel will precede the suffix as in יִשְׁמְרֵנִי *he will guard me* and שְׁלָחֵנִי *send me!* (To repeat from the discussion of נְתָנוֹ just above: in the Qal affix, when there is no affix pronoun—so this means only 3 m. sg.—an A class vowel will usually precede the suffix: קְטָלַנִי *he killed me*.

? What would קְטָלֵנִי be?_____³

4) שְׁמָרְךָ and שָׁמַרְךָ are not exactly the same. One has a meteg and one does not. The meteg denotes an open syllable, indicating that the qamats is not qamats ḥatuf. So in שְׁמָרְךָ ⁴ *he guarded you*, the qamats is an A class vowel, lengthened from the patah in שָׁמַר because it is now pretonic.

However, in שָׁמְרְךָ *to guard you*, the qamats is in a closed unaccented syllable and thus is a U class vowel. (It has been shortened from ḥolem.)

שְׁ in שְׁמָרְךָ is reduced from שָׁ due to propretonic reduction.

שָׁ in שָׁמְרְךָ is an intrinsic part of the form.

———

³ Note that the first vowel of קָטְלֵנִי is a qamats ḥatuf. (It is a qamats in a closed unaccented syllable.) When there is no suffix, this U class vowel appears between the second and third root letters קָטַל When a suffix is added, that vowel may shorten and/or move to the front of the word, yielding קָטְלֵנִי *kill me*.

⁴ For an explanation of the vocalization, see comments on 38.3 just above.

LESSON 39

—◆—

וַיְצַו מֹשֶׁה וַיַּעֲבִירוּ קוֹל בַּמַּחֲנֶה לֵאמֹר אִישׁ וְאִשָּׁה
אַל־יַעֲשׂוּ־עוֹד מְלָאכָה לִתְרוּמַת הַקֹּדֶשׁ

Exodus 36:6

S 39.1   **How can one determine whether shewa under the prefix pronoun indicates the Pi'el or is the result of reduction?**

If there is no suffix added to the verb, shortening is unlikely; in such cases shewa under the prefix pronoun will most usually indicate Pi'el. If there is a suffix, then one has to seek out other signs, such as dagesh forte in the middle root letter. If a mid- guttural—and thus no dagesh—then overall vowel pattern may help clinch the stem.

S 39.1.1   **In the case of 3rd הּ + vav conversive, could a Qal and a Pi'el ever look alike?**

Since shewa can be the vowel under the prefix pronoun in the Qal, as in וַיְהִי and the middle root letter of a Pi'el may not have dagesh forte, as in וַיְצַו such a question gives one something to think about. There is no such confusion for any of the 3rd הּ verbs in the vocabulary list because either they don't have both a Qal and a Pi'el or, if they do, the Qal is written with a different vowel: וַיֵּט for example.

?   **Review**: What are three situations that can cause dagesh forte to disappear?

1. _____

2. _____

3. _____ [1]

---

[1] 1) Shewa can make dagesh forte disappear.

2) Gutturals and ר do not take dagesh.

3) Final letters, except for ךּ do not take dagesh forte.

92

LESSON 40

גַּם עָשֹׂה תַעֲשֶׂה וְגַם יָכֹל תּוּכָל

1 Samuel 26:25

S 40.2a **Does the infinitive absolute have as many formations as the infinitive construct?**

Absolutely not! In fact, even weak verbs tend to mimic the strong vowel pattern of the infinitive absolute as in עָשֹׂה Also יָשׁוֹב→יָשֹׁב   נָגוֹשׁ→נגשׁ   קוֹם→קוּם

§ 40.2a.1 **What about the formation of the infinitive absolute in the derived stems?**

In the derived stems, the two infinitives are not so obviously distinct as they are in the Qal.

Hif`il: the only difference is that the two infinitives have different I class vowels:

הַפְקֵד (infin. absolute)   הַפְקִיד (infin. construct)

Pi`el: Two possible formations: 1) like the infinitive construct: פַּקֵּד

2) adopting the second vowel of the Qal: פַּקֹּד

Nif`al: Two possibilities, both of which show the second vowel of the Qal:

נִפְקֹד or הִפָּקֹד (compare with the infinitive construct: הִפָּקֵד)

Pu`al** and **Hof`al: Infinitive absolute is rare in these stems.

S 40.2a.2 **Does the infinitive absolute always stand before a conjugated form of the verb?**

While the most common placement of the infinitive absolute is immediately before the conjugated form of the verb and its most common function is to emphasize the idea of the verb, there are other possibilities.

1) It may be placed after the conjugated form of the verb, in which case it is thought to be less emphatic (so Joüon), or to express long continuance (Gesenius).

93

2) One idiomatic sense of the infinitive absolute—not only to express continuance but also to coordinate with another action—is seen in the use of הָלֹךְ

Jos. 6:9 וְהַמְאַסֵּף הֹלֵךְ אַחֲרֵי הָאָרוֹן הָלוֹךְ וְתָקוֹעַ בַּשּׁוֹפָרוֹת

And the rear guard was going after the ark, going and blowing the shofarot

3) The infinitive absolute may be a substitute for the finite verb:

Ex. 20:8 זָכוֹר אֶת־יוֹם הַשַּׁבָּת

Remember the Sabbath Day[1]

S 40.5 **Why does the verb יָכֹל have ḥolem in the Qal affix and shureq in the prefix?**

יָכֹל in the affix conjugates like a U class verb. (17.6c) In the prefix, one suggestion for the vowel is that יוּכַל is a Hoʻfal. But since there is no Hifʻil, that is a strained explanation. Another explanation is that it was an "old Qal passive" (see Gesenius § 53 *u* and § 69 *r* and Joüon § 75 *I*), which is also a strained explanation.

Qal Affix

		יכל	כלה	כול	אכל
sg.	3 m.	יָכֹל	כָּלָה	כָּל	אָכַל
	3 f.	יָכְלָה	כָּלְתָה	כָּלָה	אָכְלָה
	2 m.	יָכֹלְתָּ	כָּלִיתָ	כַּלְתָּ	אָכַלְתָּ
	2 f.	יָכֹלְתְּ	כָּלִית	כַּלְתְּ	אָכַלְתְּ
	1 c.	יָכֹלְתִּי	כָּלִיתִי	כַּלְתִּי	אָכַלְתִּי
pl.	3 c.	יָכְלוּ	כָּלוּ	כָּלוּ	אָכְלוּ
	2 m.	יְכָלְתֶּם	כְּלִיתֶם	כַּלְתֶּם	אֲכַלְתֶּם
	2 f.	יְכָלְתֶּן	כְּלִיתֶן	כַּלְתֶּן	אֲכַלְתֶּן
	1 c.	יָכֹלְנוּ	כָּלִינוּ	כַּלְנוּ	אָכַלְנוּ

---

[1] For more detail on the infinitive absolute see Joüon §123 and Gesenius §113.

גַּם עָשֹׂה תַעֲשֶׂה וְגַם יָכֹל תּוּכָל

Qal Prefix

sg.	3 m.	יוּכַל	יִכְלֶה	יָכוֹל	יֹאכַל
	3 f.	תּוּכַל	תִּכְלֶה	תָּכוֹל	תֹּאכַל
	2 m.	תּוּכַל	תִּכְלֶה	תָּכוֹל	תֹּאכַל
	2 f.	תּוּכְלִי	תִּכְלִי	תָּכוּלִי	תֹּאכְלִי
	1 c.	אוּכַל	אֶכְלֶה	אָכוּל	אֹכַל
pl.	3 m.	יוּכְלוּ	יִכְלוּ	יָכוּלוּ	יֹאכְלוּ
	3 f.	תּוּכַלְנָה	תִּכְלֶינָה	תָּכוֹלְנָה	תֹּאכַלְנָה
	2 m.	תּוּכְלוּ	תִּכְלוּ	תָּכוּלוּ	תֹּאכְלוּ
	2 f.	תּוּכַלְנָה	תִּכְלֶינָה	תָּכוֹלְנָה	תֹּאכַלְנָה
	1 c.	נוּכַל	נִכְלֶה	נָכוֹל	נֹאכַל

Infinitive Construct

יְכֹלֶת כְלוֹת		כוֹל	אֱכֹל

Infinitive Absolute

יָכֹל כָּלוֹה		כוֹל	אָכֹל

95

LESSON 41

נֵלְכָה־נָּא דֶּרֶךְ שְׁלֹשֶׁת יָמִים בַּמִּדְבָּר

Exodus 3:18

§ 41.2 **Is there a good source for everything you need to know about cardinals?**

Yes, two good ones at least: Gesenius § 97 and §134 and Jouön § 100.

LESSON 42

יְהִי יהוה אֱלֹהֶיךָ בָּרוּךְ

1 Kings 10:9

S 42.1a   יְהִי shows an apocopated form to indicate the jussive. **What do others look like?**

Some weak roots have a shortened vowel:

יָקָם is shortened from יָקוּם

תָּשָׁב (3 f. sg.) is shortened from תָּשׁוּב

יֵשֶׁב is shortened from יֵשֵׁב   and so on

S 42.3   **The Qal passive participle is an adjective; does that mean it is declined like a noun?**

Yes.

?   Write the Qal passive participles of בָּרךְ (Remember to adjust for propretonic reduction.)

m. sg. _____   f. sg. _____   m. pl. _____   f. pl. _____ [1]

S 42.5   **How would a sg. prefix, imperative, jussive, cohortative comparison look?**

	Prefix	Imperative		Jussive	Cohortative
strong	יִשְׁמֹר	שָׁמְרָה [2] שְׁמֹר		יִשְׁמֹר	אֶשְׁמְרָה
1st י	יֵלֵךְ	לְכָה לֵךְ		יֵלֵךְ	אֵלְכָה
1st נ	יִפֹּל	גַּשׁ נְפֹל		יִפֹּל	אֶפְּלָה
3rd ה	יַעֲשֶׂה	עֲשֵׂה		יַעַשׂ	אֶעֱשֶׂה

---

[1]   m. sg. בָּרוּךְ   f. sg. בְּרוּכָה   m. pl. בְּרוּכִים   f. pl. בְּרוּכוֹת

[2] <u>Note</u>: The syllable שָׁ — features a qamats in a closed, unaccented syllable; it is thus a qamats ḥatuf.

97

?   Write:

let us guard _____   build! (m. pl.) _____   let us fall _____

dwell (m. pl.) _____   let him answer _____   may they go _____ **3**

---

3 let us guard   נִשְׁמְרָה   build! (m. pl.)   בְּנוּ   let us fall   נִפְּלָה

dwell (m. pl.)   שְׁבוּ   let him answer   יַעַן   may they go   יֵלְכוּ

LESSON 43

וְהָיָה בִּקְרָב־אִישׁ לְהִשְׁתַּחֲוֺת לוֹ וְשָׁלַח אֶת־יָדוֹ וְהֶחֱזִיק
לוֹ וְנָשַׁק לוֹ:

2 Samuel 15:5

S 43.1   **Is context the only way to know if an affix + simple vav is expressing frequentative past?**

Yes. This lesson sentence is describing how Absolom was going about currying favor from the local inhabitants, so frequentative action in the past: *he used to . . .* or *he would . . .* is the sense of all the verbs in the verse. Even if a verb in the verse has prefix form, only context will tell you whether that is referring to the future or incomplete action in the past.

43.1.1   **Why is a qamats ḥatuf used in the first word of** בִּקְרָב־אִישׁ

Because בִּקְרָב־ is an infinitive construct in construct, its vowel is shortened. It is analogous to דָּבָר←דְּבַר except here it is a U class vowel undergoing the change: בִּקְרָב־ ← בִּקְרָב

S 43.2   לְהִשְׁתַּחֲוֺת **is distinctive enough to make recognition of the verb clear, but in its other forms does it contain any surprises?**

Yes, one: The prefix form, especially with vav conversive, is tricky. Review the discussion in the lesson and then write the following forms:

?

3 m. sg. prefix _____	3 m. sg. prefix + vav conversive _____
3 m. pl. prefix _____	3 m. pl. prefix + vav conversive _____
1 c. pl. prefix _____	m. pl. participle _____ [1]

S 43.3   **In the lesson sentence, why is the verb** וְשָׁלַח **prefixed with a** וֹ

Great question! The "conjunction" וֹ has a number of functions. In this case, it is performing two. One is grammatical: It is being used to convey repetitive action in the past.

---

[1] 3 m. sg. prefix	יִשְׁתַּחֲוֶה	
3 m. pl. prefix	יִשְׁתַּחֲווּ	
1 c. pl. prefix	נִשְׁתַּחֲוֶה	

3 m. sg. + vav conversive	וַיִּשְׁתַּחוּ
3 m. pl. + vav conversive	וַיִּשְׁתַּחֲווּ
m. pl. participle	מִשְׁתַּחֲוִים

וְהָיָה בִּקְרָב־אִישׁ לְהִשְׁתַּחֲוֺת לוֹ וְשָׁלַח אֶת־יָדוֹ וְהֶחֱזִיק לוֹ וְנָשַׁק לוֹ:

The other is syntactical, which makes this a perfect time to list the main syntactic uses of **וֹ** (The first use applies to **וְשָׁלַח**):

1) **וֹ** is often juxtaposed to the first word of a clause that follows a clause that states a time, condition, or circumstance **בִּקְרָב אִישׁ** in the lesson sentence could be either temporal or circumstantial. Other examples of this **וֹ** at work:

Genesis 22:1 וַיְהִי אַחַר הַדְּבָרִים הָאֵלֶּה וְהָאֱלֹהִים נִסָּה אֶת־אַבְרָהָם
And it happened after these things that God tested Abraham

Genesis 24:45 אֲנִי טֶרֶם אֲכַלֶּה לְדַבֵּר אֶל־לִבִּי וְהִנֵּה רִבְקָה יֹצֵאת
Even before I had finished speaking in my heart, behold, Rebecca came out . . .

Exodus 16:6 עֶרֶב וִידַעְתֶּם כִּי יהוה הוֹצִיא אֶתְכֶם מֵאֶרֶץ מִצְרָיִם
In the evening you will know that Adonai brought you from the land of Egypt

2) When an imperative is followed by an affix form + vav reversive, the affix forms take on imperative force. (But the sequence may be conveying something even stronger than the use of a string of imperatives):

1 Kings 17:2 לֵךְ מִזֶּה וּפָנִיתָ לְךָ קֵדְמָה וְנִסְתַּרְתָּ בְּנַחַל כְּרִית
Go from this (place) and turn east and hide in the Wadi of K'rit

3) When an imperative, cohortative, or jussive is followed by **וֹ** + prefix form, the prefix form is thought to convey purpose or result:

1 Kings 17: 10 וַיֹּאמֶר קְחִי־נָא לִי מְעַט־מַיִם בַּכְּלִי וְאֶשְׁתֶּה
And he said, "Bring me, please, a little water in the vessel that I may drink"

4) **וֹ** can introduce the apodosis (the "then" clause of a conditional sentence):

Exodus 19:5 וְעַתָּה אִם־שָׁמוֹעַ תִּשְׁמְעוּ בְּקֹלִי . . . וִהְיִיתֶם לִי סְגֻלָּה
And now, if you will listen, listen to my voice . . . then you will be to me a treasure

5) **וֹ** can function to specify something and be translated *even* or *that is*:

וּשְׁמוּאֵל מֵת וַיִּסְפְּדוּ־לוֹ כָּל־יִשְׂרָאֵל וַיִּקְבְּרֻהוּ בָרָמָה וּבְעִירוֹ
1 Samuel 28:3
And Samuel died, and all Israel mourned him, and they buried him in Ramah, that is, in his city

וְהָיָה בִּקְרָב־אִישׁ לְהִשְׁתַּחֲוֺת לוֹ וְשָׁלַח אֶת־יָדוֹ וְהֶחֱזִיק לוֹ וְנָשַׁק לוֹ:

6) When there is a change in subject or scene, וֹ on a noun, proper noun, or pronoun can express contrast:

Genesis 37:11 וַיְקַנְאוּ־בוֹ אֶחָיו וְאָבִיו שָׁמַר אֶת־הַדָּבָר:

<u>*And his brothers were jealous of him, but his father guarded the matter*</u>

In that same chapter, see verses 22 and 24 for two other examples.

7) וֹ can be put between words or sentences to show their resemblance:

וְאִם־לֹא תִשְׁמְעוּ בְּקוֹל יְהוָה... וְהָיְתָה יַד־יְהוָה בָּכֶם וּבַאֲבֹתֵיכֶם

1 Samuel 12:15

And if you will not listen to the voice of Adonai, then <u>the hand of Adonai will be against you</u>
<u>*(as it was) against your fathers*</u>

8) Sometimes initial וֹ is plain "and:"

Genesis 37:10 הֲבוֹא נָבוֹא אֲנִי וְאִמְּךָ וְאַחֶיךָ לְהִשְׁתַּחֲוֺת לְךָ אָרְצָה

Shall we come, I <u>and your mother and your brothers</u>, to prostrate ourselves
in worship to you on the ground?

9) Sometimes the meaning of וֹ remains controversial:

Song of Songs 1:5 שְׁחוֹרָה אֲנִי וְנָאוָה

I am dark <u>and</u> comely
I am dark <u>but</u> comely

LESSON 44

אַתָּה הָרְאֵתָ לָדַעַת כִּי יְהוָה הוּא הָאֱלֹהִים אֵין עוֹד מִלְבַדּוֹ׃

Deuteronomy 4:35

S 44.1   Since gutturals can cause vowel changes, how could one know that הָרְאֵתָ is not a Hif'il?

הָרְאֵתָ shown accented, reveals that the initial qamats is in a closed, unaccented syllable (qamats ḥatuf). Therefore it is a reduced U class vowel. Though the Hif'il can show qamats under a preformative ה (in the imperative or infinitive of a hollow verb, לְהָקִים e.g.) it will not be in a closed, unaccented syllable.

S44.2   **Review** In לָדַעַת why is the ל pointed לָ not לִ

?   (S 11.2)

S 44.8   הוֹדַע does not have an I class vowel between the second and third root letters. Can it still be a Hif'il?

Yes, but it can also be a Ho'fal. If a Hif'il, the guttural ע is attracting the vowel pataḥ. This does not always happen with 3rd gutturals, but it can, especially with ע The initial ____ הוֹ is all that is left to give the information, "Hif'il of a 1st י " If a Ho'fal—as in Leviticus 4:23—it is a variant spelling of הוּדַע

LESSON 45

וָאֶ֫עַשׂ בַּבֹּ֫קֶר כַּאֲשֶׁר צֻוֵּ֫יתִי

Ezekiel 24:18

S 45.1
?

Review In וָאֶ֫עַשׂ why is the ו pointed וָ?

_____ (14.5a)

S 45.2
?

Review Why there is a dagesh in the second בּ of בַּבֹּ֫קֶר

_____ (38.2a)

S45.2.1
?

Review Why is the vowel under the כּ of כַּאֲשֶׁר not shewa?

_____ **(S 14.3.1)**

S 45.3
?

Review In צֻוֵּ֫יתִי how do you know that the dot in ו is a dagesh?

_____ (37.2a)

S 45.3.1   **When the middle root letter of a Pu`al cannot take dagesh, what is the compensatory vowel change?**

Shureq ‌ֻ lengthens to ḥolem וֹ

Middle letter containing dagesh צֻוֵּ֫יתִי   Compensatory lengthening בֹּרַ֫כְתִּי

Middle letter containing dagesh אֲגֻלֶּה   Compensatory lengthening אֲבֹרַךְ

S 45.3.2   **How does one distinguish the Pu`al from the Hof`al?**

The Pu`al, being the passive of the Pi`el, is also distinguished by having dagesh forte in the middle root letter. Also, in the prefix form, both the Pi`el and the Pu`al have shewa under the prefix pronoun.

The Ho`fal affix, like the Hif`il, has a ה preformative. In the prefix, the distinction is a bit more subtle, being based on a vowel distinction under the prefix pronoun.

פֻּקַּ֫דְנוּ   Pu`al affix          הׇפְקַ֫דְנוּ   Hof`al affix

נְפֻקַּד   Pu`al prefix          נׇפְקַד   Hof`al prefix

103

S 45.5   **What is the difference between a preposition alone and a preposition+אֲשֶׁר**

A preposition alone introduces a phrase. A preposition + אֲשֶׁר introduces a clause.

כְּ	_like_ or _as_	כָּאֵלֶּה	_like these_	כַּאֲשֶׁר צִוָּה אֱלֹהִים	_as God commanded_
עַד	_until_	עַד הַיּוֹם	_until today_	עַד אֲשֶׁר יִרְאֶה	_until he should see_

LESSON 46

◆

וְרָאוּ כָּל־עַמֵּי הָאָרֶץ כִּי שֵׁם יהוה נִקְרָא עָלֶיךָ

Deuteronomy 28:10

S 46.7a The Nif`al affix of 1st י verbs begins נוֹ  The Hif`il affix begins הוֹ Is the reason the same?

Yes. In both cases, the weak 1st י is affected by the stem preformative, which causes the י to revert to its original ו

	Hif`il Affix		
strong verb	הִפְקִיד	1st י	הוֹדִיעַ

	Nif`il Affix		
strong verb	נִפְקַד	1st י	נוֹדַע

S 46.7a.1 Are there other morphological similarities between the Hif`il affix and the Nif`al affix?

Yes. 1st gutturals are affected similarly by the attachment of a stem preformative:

	Hif`il Affix		
strong verb	הִפְקִיד	1st guttural	הֶעֱמִיד

	Nif`al Affix		
strong verb	נִפְקַד	1st guttural	נֶעֱמַד

Hollows also show similar responses to a stem preformative in terms of the preformative's causing, at the very least, vowel changes. In the second and first persons, they both have an extra syllable before the affix pronoun and consequently a reduced vowel under the preformative. Using קוּם as an example:

Hif`il Affix

strong verb	הִפְקִיד	hollow 3 m. sg.	הֵקִים
		2 m. sg.	הֲקִימוֹתָ

Nif`al Affix

strong verb	נִפְקַד	hollow 3 m. sg.	נָקוֹם
		2 m. sg.	נְקוּמוֹתָ

LESSON 47

וַעֲשֵׂה־שָׁם מִזְבֵּחַ לָאֵל הַנִּרְאֶה אֵלֶיךָ

Genesis 35:1

S 47.1   **What can a הָ ending on a word indicate?**

?

a)   If the word is a verb, הָ indicates the m. sg. imperative: בְּנֵה עֲלֵה עֲשֵׂה
What is the ending of 3rd ה prefix forms that have no prefix complement? _____ 1

b)   If the word is a noun, הָ indicates the m. sg. construct: שְׂדֵה־מוֹאָב
What would be the m. sg. absolute of שְׂדֵה־ _____ 2

?   Write the following verbs:

a)   3 m. sg. Nif`al affix: he was found: _____

b)   m. sg. Nif`al participle: found _____

c)   3 m. sg. Nif`al affix: he appeared _____

d)   m. sg. Nif`al participle: appearing/seen _____

e)   3 m. sg. Nif`al affix: he was guarded _____

f)   m. sg. Nif`al participle: guarded _____ 3

---

¹ הָ (Example: תַּעֲשֶׂה)

² שָׂדֶה

³ a) נִמְצָא   b) נִמְצָא   c) נִרְאָה   d) נִרְאָה   e) נִשְׁמַר   f) נִשְׁמָר

LESSON 48

וְלֹא־יִשָּׁמַע בָּהּ עוֹד קוֹל בְּכִי

Isaiah 65:19

S 48.1   **The Nif`al seems to be less patterned than other stems. Is it?**

Somewhat. In most stems the prefix form sets the vowel pattern for the imperative, participle, and infinitive. In the Nif`al, the prefix vowel pattern is seen in the imperative and the infinitive but not in the participle. (47.2)

S 48.3   **בְּכִי** *weeping* looks structurally like **שְׁמִי** *my name*. **How can that be?**

There are a few two-letter nouns, like **שֵׁם** that, when a 1 c. sg. suffix is added, are patterned like **שְׁמִי** One you know well is **בְּן ← בְּנִי** Confusion comes in because 3rd ה roots tend to yield 3rd י nouns, **בְּכִי** from **בכה** for example (see 48.7). When that sort of noun has a 1 c. sg. suffix, it usually takes another י to represent the suffix as in **בִּכְיִי** *my weeping*.[1] One has to know the history of the word to be able to tell what ◌ִ◌ is. Making things a little worse is the f. sg. imperative of weak roots, which could have the same pattern, for example, **עֲלִי גְּשִׁי תְּנִי**

48.5b   **Identify the stem of each of the following words:**

?

תַּגַּע _____	תִּנָּגַע _____	תְּנַגַּע _____	תְּנֻגַּע _____
תַּגִּיעַ _____	תֻּגַּע _____	תּוֹלִיד _____	תִּוָּלֵד _____
תּוֹלַד _____	תֵּלֶד _____	תְּיַלֵּד _____	מְיַלֶּדֶת _____ [2]

---

[1] The word **פֶּה** which is actually a one-consonant noun, is ambiguous in its construct and 1. c. sg. suffixed forms: **פִּי** can be either *mouth of* or *my mouth*.

[2] תַּגַּע Qal	תִּנָּגַע Nif`al	תְּנַגַּע Pi`el	תְּנֻגַּע Pu`al
תַּגִּיעַ Hif`il	תֻּגַּע Hof`al	תּוֹלִיד Hif`il	תִּוָּלֵד Nif`al
תּוֹלַד Hof`al	תֵּלֶד Qal	תְּיַלֵּד Pi`el	מְיַלֶּדֶת Pi`el

LESSON 49

וַיֹּאמֶר אֵלַי הִנָּבֵא אֶל־הָרוּחַ הִנָּבֵא בֶן־אָדָם

Ezekiel 37:9

S 49.2   **How does the Nifʿal come to have a הַ in the preformative of some forms?**

There are some creative but not especially convincing answers to that question. Gesenius, for example, calls the הַ in the imperative and infinitive a secondary addition (see Gesenius § 51*a*). The הַ is disconcerting, but the ◌ַ ◌ְ ◌ָ or ◌ִ ◌ְ ◌ָ vowel pattern should help identify a Nifʿal.

S 49.2.1   **When the Nifʿal begins with הַ how can one distinguish it from a Hifʿil?**

The vowel patterns will be different. Both could begin הַ (the Hifʿil in the affix and the Nifʿal in the infinitive and imperative). But then the patterns become distinctive.

?   All the words below begin with הַ Identify the stem.

הָאָמֵר	_____	הוֹדַע	_____	הִשָּׁמֵר	_____	הִשְׁמִיד	_____
¹הֻגַּד	_____	הוֹלְכִים	_____	הוֹדִעֵנִי	_____		

---

¹Hifʿil	הִשְׁמִיד	Nifʿal	הִשָּׁמֵר	Nifʿal	הוֹדַע	Nifʿal	הָאָמֵר
Hifʿil	הוֹדִעֵנִי	Qal	הוֹלְכִים	Hofʿal	הֻגַּד		

109

LESSON 50

וַיֹּסֶף יהוה לְהֵרָאֹה בְשִׁלֹה

1 Samuel 3:21

S 50.2   Translate:

?

	הַמֶּלֶךְ		נִמְלַךְ		הַמָּלֵךְ
	הוּשֵׁב		נִבְנֶה		הִבָּנֹה
	נוֹשַׁב		נִבְנוּ		נֵשֵׁב
	הִמְלִיךְ		הַמֹּלֵךְ		הוֹשִׁיב [1]

---

[1]

(cause to become) king	הַמָּלֵךְ	he was made king	נִמְלַךְ	become king	הַמָּלֵךְ
be seated	הוּשֵׁב	we will build	נִבְנֶה	be built	הִבָּנֹה
he was seated	נוֹשַׁב	they were built	נִבְנוּ	we will sit/dwell	נֵשֵׁב
he caused to rule	הִמְלִיךְ	the one ruling	הַמֹּלֵךְ	he seated	הוֹשִׁיב

110

LESSON 51

◆

וָאֵסָב אֶת־הַר־שֵׂעִיר יָמִים רַבִּים

Deuteronomy 2:1

S 51   **Despite their irregularities, geminates seem to have the most in common with hollows. Do they?**

Yes. In fact, both hollows and geminates tend to yield two-letter nouns. To read more about roots, see James Barr's *Comparative Philology*, 166–70.

LESSON 52

— ◆ —

אֵ֫לֶּה אֲשֶׁר שָׁלַח יהוה לְהִתְהַלֵּךְ בָּאָ֫רֶץ

Zechariah 1:10

S 52.2   **The Hitpaʿel looks easy to recognize. Does this stem contain any surprises?**

One or two. One is that when a root begins with a sibilant, that is, ז שׁ שׂ ס צ the sibilant and the preformative element ת change places (metathesize). So, for example, הִשְׁתַּמֵּר → הִתְשַׁמֵּר The other is that when the middle root letter is a guttural, there will be lengthening of the preceding vowel to compensate: הִתְבָּרֵךְ for example, or put another way, the changes that a mid-guttural or ר would cause in the Piʿel they will also cause in the Hitpaʿel.

LESSON 53

וַיִּתְהַלֵּךְ חֲנוֹךְ אֶת־הָאֱלֹהִים וְאֵינֶנּוּ כִּי־לָקַח אֹתוֹ אֱלֹהִים:

Genesis 5:24

§ 53.5a **How is it that נּוּ can be both *him* and *us*?**

That נּוּ can and does mean *us* is not surprising. That it can mean *him* needs some explaining. The full spelling for the 3 m. sg. suffix with energic נ is נְהוּ (preserved in Ex. 15:2: וַאֲרֹמְמֶנְהוּ *and I will exalt him*). But the ה of נְהוּ usually elides, leaving us with נּוּ That makes sense, doesn't it? Context is usually quite clear as to which of the two pronouns is meant.

Plain נוּ does not have that ambiguity. It has another. It can be the affix subject pronoun "we" or the object suffix "us." You will have to depend on vowel patterns and context to determine whether it is subject or object.

LESSON 54

———

בִּשְׁנַת עֶשְׂרִים וָשֶׁבַע שָׁנָה לְיָרָבְעָם מֶלֶךְ יִשְׂרָאֵל מָלַךְ עֲזַרְיָה
בֶן־אֲמַצְיָה מֶלֶךְ יְהוּדָה: בֶּן־שֵׁשׁ עֶשְׂרֵה שָׁנָה הָיָה בְמָלְכוֹ
וַחֲמִשִּׁים וּשְׁתַּיִם שָׁנָה מָלַךְ בִּירוּשָׁלָ͏ם

2 Kings 15:1–2

S 54   **Are the ordinals related to the cardinals?**

The ordinals from 2 through 10 are formed from the cardinals and have the endings
יִ◌ (m.) יִת◌ (f.). There are two irregularities. "First" is רִאשׁוֹן (m.) רִאשׁוֹנָה (f.),
and the word for "fourth" רְבִעִי does not have the prosthetic (extra) א of אַרְבַּע

114

VOCABULARY

EXERCISES

Lesson 1

Particles and words 1–10

בֵּן	7	וְ	1
עָלָה	8	כִּי	2
בְּ	9	הָיָה	3
לְ	10	אֲשֶׁר	4
עָלָה	11	אֶל	5
לֹא	12	בַּת	6

Lesson 2

Words 1–20

בָּא	8	מַעֲשֶׂה	1
יוֹמוֹ	9	וַיֹּאמֶר לוֹט	2
פָּנָה	10	כּוֹל	3
בֵּיתוֹ	11	אֶל אֶרֶץ	4
בּוֹ	12	עָשָׂה יהוה	5
בָּנָיו	13	בְּנוֹ	6
בּוֹא	14	מַמְלָכָה	7

Lesson 3

Words 1–30

6	אֶל עַמּוֹ	1	וַיִּשְׁמַע יוֹסֵף
7	עָשָׂה יִצְחָק	2	מִמִּדְבָּר
8	נָתַן אֱלֹהִים לוֹ	3	בְּיָדוֹ
9	הִיא	4	רָאָה מַרְאֶה
10	פָּנָיו	5	וַיֵּלֶךְ שָׁאוּל

Lesson 4

Words 1–40

7	לֹא לָקַח	1	הִנֵּה בַת
8	מֵעַל	2	וַיֵּשֶׁב הָאָב עִמּוֹ
9	בַּיִת אֶחָד	3	עַד מוֹאָב
10	אֵלֶּה	4	וַיֵּצֵא יִצְחָק
11	שׁוּב	5	שָׁב הָאִישׁ אֶל עִירוֹ
12	זֶה הוּא	6	מָלַךְ הָאִישׁ כִּי מֶלֶךְ הָיָה

Lesson 5

Words 1–50

8	עָלָיו	1	אֲנִי לֹא מָרְדֳּחַי
9	מוֹתוֹ	2	וַיִּשְׁלַח
10	זֹאת	3	בְּיַד יהוה

4 וַיִּשְׁמַע וַיֵּדַע

11 שָׁנָה

5 עֲבַד אֵלִיָּהוּ

12 אֲשֶׁר לֹא עָבַד

6 פָּנִים אֶל פָּנִים

13 שָׁב

7 שְׁמוֹ שִׁמְשׁוֹן

14 מֵת

Lesson 6

Words 1–60

1 עֵינֵי כָּל־יִשְׂרָאֵל עָלָיו

2 וַיָּמֻתוּ

3 אָכַל

4 מַה וְלָמָּה

5 שְׁנַיִם

6 אַתָּה הָאִישׁ וְגַם כֹּהֵן

7 וַיֵּדְעוּ כָּל־הַמְּלָכִים

8 וַיָּבֹאוּ עַבְדֵי אַבְשָׁלוֹם אֶל־הָאִשָּׁה

9 הִנֵּה הָאָב אֲשֶׁר לֹא אָמַר דָּבָר אֶל בְּנוֹ

10 שָׁם and שֵׁם אִם שָׁם and עִם

VOCABULARY

Lesson 7

Words 1–70

1 אַתֶּם

2 דַּרְכֵי צִיּוֹן

3 נַפְשׁוֹ

4 הָאֲחֵרִים

5 וַיֵּשֶׁב אֶל הַמָּקוֹם וַיִּקְרָא שָׁם בְּשֵׁם יהוה

6 אֲנִי הָרִאשׁוֹן

7 כַּאֲחוֹת

8 אַחַר

9 לָכֵן

10 קָם

11 רָאָה אֶת הָרָעָה

12 וַיִּשָּׂא אַבְרָהָם אֶת עֵינָיו

13 אֵין כֹּהֲנִים בְּבֵית־יהוה

Lesson 8

Words 1–80

1 כֹּה אָמַר יהוה

2 מֵאָה

3 אָדָם הוּא מִן הָאֲדָמָה

4 כָּל־גּוֹיֵי הָאָרֶץ

120

5 וַיָּשֶׂם דָּוִד אֶת־הַדְּבָרִים... בִּלְבָבוֹ

6 וַיָּקָם וַיֵּלֶךְ אֶל רֹאשׁ הָהָר

7 כִּי זֶה אֲדֹנִי

Lesson 9

Words 1–90

1 אֵין מַיִם

2 קוֹל קֹרֵא

3 עַמּוּדֵי־הַבַּיִת

4 תַּחְתָּיו

5 חָיָה

6 לֹא יָשְׁבוּ הָעֲבָדִים כִּי אַתֶּם קָמִים

7 וַיֵּצֵא וְעָבַר אֶל הָהָר

8 אֶלֶף וּמֵאָה

9 רֹאשִׁי

10 וַיִּגְדַּל

11 עֶשְׂרִים

12 יֶלֶד

13 עוֹד יוֹסֵף חַי

(treat as an interrogative noun sentence)

VOCABULARY

Lesson 10

Words 1–100

1   קָדוֹשׁ אֲנִי לָכֵן אַתָּה קָדוֹשׁ

2   וְעָבְדוּ הֵם אֶת יהוה לְעוֹלָם

3   צִוָּה יהוה אֶת דָּוִד אֲשֶׁר הָלַךְ עִם הַצָּבָא

4   וַיִּקְרָא הַשֹּׁמֵר אֶל הָעָנִי הַיּוֹשֵׁב בְּבֵית יהוה

5   עַתָּה הָעֵת

6   לְמַעַן הַמִּצְוָה

7   וְשָׁמַר יהוה אֶת־דְּרָכַי

8   וַיִּמְצְאוּ שָׁם אֶת שָׁאוּל

9   מִי הָאִישׁ אֲשֶׁר לֹא עָבַר אֶת הַיַּרְדֵּן

10   פִּי הַמֶּלֶךְ

Lessons 11–12

Words 1–110

1   וַיְהִי כֵן

2   וַיַּעַן וַיֹּאמֶר

3   הִיא בְּכָל־נְשִׂיאֵי יִשְׂרָאֵל

4   הַשָּׂר הַגָּדֹל

5   שְׁלֹשָׁה כֹהֲנִים

6   וַיֵּלְכוּ פַרְעֹה וְכָל־מִצְרַיִם בְּתוֹךְ הַיָּם (sea ←— יָם)

7   עָשָׂה יהוה אֶת הַשָּׁמַיִם וְאֵת הָאָרֶץ

8   וַיִּקַּח גָּלְיָת אֶת־חַרְבּוֹ בְּיָדוֹ וַיֹּאמֶר מִי הָאִישׁ אֲשֶׁר לוֹ רַב כֶּסֶף וְאֵין

אָמַר דָּבָר (silver ⟶ כֶּסֶף)

9   מִי אַתָּה בְּנִי

10   וַיִּשְׁפֹּט הַשֹּׁפֵט אֶת עַמִּי יִשְׂרָאֵל

11   עֵת לָלֶדֶת וְעֵת לָמוּת

12   יָרֵא הָאִישׁ אֶת־אֲדֹנִי הַמֶּלֶךְ

Lessons 13–14

Words 1–120

1   וָאֵרֶד

2   גָּדַלְנוּ

3   רְאוֹת

4   לָרֶדֶת

5   תִּשְׁלַחְנָה

6   נַעֲבֹד

7   תַּחַת הָעֵיצִים

8   שְׁנֵי נְעָרָיו

9   אֵשׁ־יהוה נָפְלָה מִן הַשָּׁמַיִם

10   יִמְלֹךְ יהוה לְעוֹלָם

11   וַתִּשָּׂא רוּחַ אֶת יְחֶזְקֵאל וַיָּבֹא יְרוּשָׁלְָמָה

12   וַתִּגְדַּל בַּת־הַמֶּלֶךְ וַיִּתֶּן לָהּ אָבִיהָ בָּקָר וַתֹּאמֶר מָה זֶה אַתָּה נָתַן לִי

13   וַיִּזְבְּחוּ זְבָחִים עַל הַמִּזְבֵּחַ

14 וַיֵּלְכוּ שְׁנֵיהֶם יַחְדָּו

15 חָיָה וַיָּ֫מָת

Lessons 15–16

Words 1–130

תַּעֲבֹדְנָה	9	אֵין דָּם עַל יָדִי	1
אָבַ֫לְתָּ	10	חֲמִשָּׁה מַלְאָכִים	2
הַיּוֹם הַשְּׁלִישִׁי	11	יָשְׁבָה בָּאֹהֱלָה	3
בֵּרַ֫כְתִּי	12	אֵ֫לֶּה רָאשֵׁי הַגּוֹיִם	4
מַיִם חַיִּים	13	אַיִל אֶחָד	5
וַתָּ֫שֶׂם	14	שָׁנָה טוֹבָה	6
זַרְעוֹ	15	שַׁ֫עַר הַשָּׁמַיִם	7
מִי אָהֵב אִשָּׁה רָעָה	16	וַיִּ֫בֶן שָׁם מִזְבֵּחַ	8

Lessons 17–18

Words 1–140

וְנָתַתָּ לִי לֶחֶם 1

שִׁבְעָה אֵלִים · בָּאִים 2

גָּדְלָה הַמִּלְחָמָה 3

אַרְבָּעִים אֲבָנִים 4

הַשֶּׁ֫מֶשׁ הִיא בַּשָּׁמַיִם 5

6 וּמֵת הָאִישׁ אֲשֶׁר־שָׁכַב עִמָּהּ

7 יִרְאָתָן

8 הַמַּלְאָךְ נָגַע בּוֹ

9 עֲזָבוּנוּ

10 הָאֶבֶן אֲשֶׁר שָׁם יַעֲקֹב הָיָה כְּעַמּוּד

Lessons 19–20

Words 1–150

1 צָפֹנָה וָנֶגְבָּה

2 תֵּצְאוּ לְמִלְחָמָה עַל־אֹיְבֶיךָ

3 עָשָׂה יהוה אֶת הַיָּם

4 אוֹיְבִי לֹא יָשׁוּב אֶל אָבִיו

5 מִן־הַמִּשְׁפָּחָה הָרָעָה הַזֹּאת

6 כַּעֲפַר הָאָרֶץ

7 וַתִּקְרַבְנָה לִפְנֵי אֶלְעָזָר הַכֹּהֵן

8 בְּקִרְבִּי

9 בִּגְדֵי קֹדֶשׁ הֵם

10 וַיִּפֶן יָמָּה

11 וַתִּלְבַּשׁ אֶסְתֵּר מַלְכוּת

VOCABULARY

◆

Lessons 21–22

Words 1–160

1 לֹא כֵן הָרְשָׁעִים

2 אָסְפָה רָחֵל אֶת הַצֹּאן אֲשֶׁר לְאָבִיהָ

3 קַח מַטְּךָ וּנְטֵה־יָדְךָ עַל מֵימֵי מִצְרַיִם

4 יָד תַּחַת יָד רֶגֶל תַּחַת רָגֶל

5 יָבֹאוּ אַחֲרֵיהֶם פַּרְעֹה וְכָל־חֵילוֹ בְּתוֹךְ הַיָּם

6 הַיָּם מָלֵא מַיִם

7 תִּשְׁכַּב עַל מִטָּתְךָ הַלַּיְלָה הַזֶּה

8 וְלָקְחוּ אֲבָנִים אֲחֵרוֹת

9 תְּנִי־לִי לֶחֶם וּבָשָׂר

10 כִּי־גָדֹל עַד שָׁמַיִם חַסְדֶּךָ

Lessons 23–24

Words 1–170

1 יָכוֹל

2 כְּתֹב אֶל אִמְּךָ וְאֶל אָבִיךָ

3 בַּקֵּשׁ וְתִמְצָא

4 ... וַיָּמָת לִבּוֹ בְּקִרְבּוֹ וְהוּא הָיָה לְאָבֶן:

5 חַוָּה הִיא אֵם כָּל־חָי

6 זָכַר הַנֹּעַר

7 חֶסֶד וְשָׁלוֹם וְחַיִל

8 אֲנַחְנוּ שָׁמַעְנוּ כִּי רַבּוּ הָאֹיְבִים וּבְנֵיהֶם יָרְשׁוּ אֶת גְּבוּלֵינוּ

9 וְהִנֵּה רָחֵל בָּאָה עִם הַצֹּאן אֲשֶׁר לְאָבִיהָ

10 אַל־תִּגְּשׁוּ אֶל־אִשָּׁא

Lessons 25–26

Words 1–180

1 קוֹל נָתְנוּ בְּבֵית־יהוה כְּיוֹם מוֹעֵד

2 עֵת לִשְׁתּוֹת אוֹ עֵת לֶאֱכֹל

3 עֲזֻבָה

4 שַׂר הַשָּׂר וַיֵּצֵא

5 וַיְהִי בֹקֶר

6 אַרְבַּע חָמֵשׁ שֵׁשׁ

7 תּוֹרוֹתֶיךָ

8 מַלְאָכִי

9 יֶאֱהַב

10 עֲדַת־יִשְׂרָאֵל

11 עָבַדְתָּ וְלֹא אָבַדְתָּ

12 הַמֶּלֶךְ יִכְתָּב־לוֹ תּוֹרָה

VOCABULARY

Lessons 27–28

Words 1–190

Four roots not extant in Qal: (verb)　　1　יֵשַׁע נֵצֵל כּוּן שֶׁבַע

Four words with some or all of the same letters:　　2　מֵאָה מָה אִם אָמָה

3　מַחֲנֵה לְוִיִּם

4　קַח אֶת־אַהֲרֹן וְאֶת־בָּנָיו... וְאֵת הַבְּגָדִים

5　וְאָסַפְתִּי אוֹתָם אֶל־תּוֹךְ הָעִיר

6　אִישׁ צַדִּיק מִי יִמְצָא

7　וְאֶת־הַכֵּלִים שָׁם בְּאָהֳלוֹ

8　לְמַעַן דַּעַת דֹּרוֹת בְּנֵי־יִשְׂרָאֵל

9　וְהַמֶּלֶךְ דָּוִד זָקֵן

10　וַתָּבוֹא אֵלָיו וַיִּשְׁכַּב עִמָּהּ

11　פְּקָד־נָא

12　חַטָּאת חָטָא

13　לְסֵפֶת

14　וְהָרָשָׁע כִּי יָשׁוּב מִכָּל־חַטֹּאתָיו אֲשֶׁר עָשָׂה

15　נֶחֱנֶה

16　וַיְכַל אֱלֹהִים מְלַאכְתּוֹ אֲשֶׁר עָשָׂה

Lessons 29–30

Words 1–200

1   כָּלְתָה הָרָעָה

2   וּכְבוֹדִי לְאַחֵר לֹא־אֶתֵּן

3   שָׁמְנִים טוֹבִים

4   שָׂנְאוּ אֹתוֹ אֲחֵי יוֹסֵף

5   וְעַתָּה יָרוּם רֹאשִׁי עַל אֹיְבַי

6   וָאָשִׂים נַפְשִׁי בְכַפִּי

7   הֲלוֹא אַחֶיךָ רֹעִים בִּשְׁכֶם

8   אָזְנַיִם לִשְׁמֹעַ עֵינַיִם לִרְאוֹת וְרַגְלַיִם לָלֶכֶת נָתַן לָנוּ אֱלֹהִים

9   וְגִלִּיתִי אֶת־לִבָּךְ

10   אֵלִיָּהוּ הַנָּבִיא

11   וַתִּכְבַּד הַמִּלְחָמָה עַל־שָׁאוּל

12   וַיִּקַּח שְׁלֹשָׁה שְׁבָטִים בְּכַפּוֹ

Lessons 31–32

Words 1–210

1   וְיָרְשׁוּ אֶת־שְׂדֵה אֶפְרַיִם

2   הַיּוֹתֵר

3   בָּחַר בָּנוּ לִהְיוֹת לוֹ גּוֹי קָדוֹשׁ

4   וַיִּחַן שָׁם יִשְׂרָאֵל נֶגֶד הָהָר

5   לֵךְ וְאָסַפְתָּ אֶת־זִקְנֵי יִשְׂרָאֵל

6   וַיִּבֶן אֵלִי כִּי יְהוָה קֹרֵא לַנַּעַר

עַל שְׂפַת הַיָּם 7

שַׁאֲלוּ שְׁלוֹם יְרוּשָׁלַ͏ִם 8

דּוֹר הֹלֵךְ וְדוֹר בָּא וְהָאָרֶץ לְעוֹלָם עֹמָדֶת: 9

רַב הַמָּקוֹם בֵּינֵיהֶם 10

כְּתֹב זֹאת בַּסֵּפֶר 11

קַח אֶת־בֶּהֱמַת הַלְוִיִּם תַּחַת בְּהֶמְתָּם 12

בְּמִסְפַּר שִׁבְטֵי יִשְׂרָאֵל 13

Lessons 33–34

Words 1–220

מִחוּץ לַמַּחֲנֶה 1

לְהָבִין בֵּין־טוֹב לָרָע 2

וְהָרַגְתִּי אֶתְכֶם בֶּחָרֶב 3

וְהוּא יֹשֵׁב פֶּתַח־הָאֹהֶל 4

תָּבוֹא הִיא סָבִיב הָהָר 5

וְלֹא־תִקְרְאִי־לִי עוֹד בַּעְלִי 6

וְנָסְנוּ לִפְנֵיהֶם וְיִסְעוּ אֶל אֲדוֹנִי 7

אַל־תִּשְׁפֹּךְ דָּם 8

וְחַטָּאתָם כִּי כָבְדָה מְאֹד 9

כִּי לֹא־עָזַבְתָּ דֹרְשֶׁיךָ יהוה 10

וְאִם־לֹא הַגִּידוּ לִי 11

130

EXERCISES

Lessons 35–36

Words 1–230

1 גִּבּוֹר חַיִל וְאִישׁ מִלְחָמָה

2 מִי־כָמֹכָה יהוה

3 שְׁאַל אָבִיךָ וְיַגֵּדְךָ

4 וַתִּיטַב הַנַּעֲרָה בְּעֵינָיו

5 וְעָשִׂיתָ כְּחָכְמָתֶךָ

6 מִי שָׂם פֶּה לָאָדָם

7 כִּי רָעָה אָנֹכִי מֵבִיא מִצָּפוֹן

8 יִשְׂמְחוּ הַשָּׁמַיִם

9 וְזֹאת תּוֹרַת הַמִּנְחָה

10 אֵלֶּה הַחֻקִּים אֲשֶׁר מְצַוֶּה יהוה אֶתְכֶם הַיּוֹם

11 וַיַּחֲנוּ בְנֵי־יִשְׂרָאֵל נֶגְדָּם

12 וַיָּרֶם מֹשֶׁה אֶת־יָדוֹ וַיַּךְ אֶת־הַסֶּלַע (rock)

13 אֲנִי לְבַדִּי דְּרֶשֶׁת אֶת־יהוה לְהַקְרִיב עֹלוֹת אֵילִים מָאתַיִם

14 יְדַבֵּר אֲדֹנִי כִּי חִזַּקְתָּנִי

Lessons 37–38

Words 1–240

1 נָסַע וְלֹא נָס

2 וַיּוֹסִפוּ עוֹד שְׂנֹא אֹתוֹ

3 יַיִן לֹא שָׁתִיתִי

4 שָׁבְרִי רֶגֶל

5   הֲלֹא מֵאָז הִשְׁמַעְתִּיךָ

6   הַלְלוּ אֶת־שֵׁם יהוה הַלְלוּ עַבְדֵי יהוה:

7   שֶׁעֹמְדִים בְּבֵת יהוה בְּחַצְרוֹת בֵּית אֱלֹהֵינוּ:

8   לֹא אַשְׁחִית אִם־אֶמְצָא שָׁם אַרְבָּעִים וַחֲמִשָּׁה

9   כִּי תָנוּחַ יַד־יהוה בָּהָר הַזֶּה

10   כִּי־יָצָא הָאֱלֹהִים לְפָנֶיךָ לְהַכּוֹת אֶת־מַחֲנֵה פְלִשְׁתִּים

11   וְלֹא הֶאֱמַנְתֶּם לוֹ

12   כִּי־כָלִינוּ בְאַפֶּךָ

13   לָלֶכֶת לְפָנַי בֶּאֱמֶת

14   לָמָּה שְׁכַחְתָּנִי

Lessons 39–40

Words 1–250

1   פִּתְחוּ לִי שַׁעֲרֵי־צֶדֶק

2   יְמִין יהוה עֹשָׂה חָיִל

3   תִּבְנֶה חוֹמוֹת יְרוּשָׁלִָם

4   רְדוּ לִקְרַאת מִדְיָן

5   מַה־טֹּבוּ אֹהָלֶיךָ יַעֲקֹב מִשְׁכְּנֹתֶיךָ יִשְׂרָאֵל:

6   וְהָיָה כְּשִׁבְתּוֹ עַל כִּסֵּא מַמְלַכְתּוֹ

7   וַיִּשְׁכֹּן כְּבוֹד־יהוה עַל־הַר סִינַי

8   צֶדֶק צֶדֶק תִּרְדֹּף

9   הֲיֵשׁ יהוה בְּקִרְבֵּנוּ אִם־אָיִן

10   לְכָל־כֵּלָיו תַּעֲשֶׂה נְחֹשֶׁת

11   וַיֹּאמֶר יְהוֹשָׁפָט אֶל־מֶלֶךְ יִשְׂרָאֵל כָּמוֹנִי כָמוֹךָ כְּעַמִּי כְעַמֶּךָ כְּסוּסַי כְּסוּסֶיךָ

12   אִישׁ בְּנַחֲלַת מַטֵּה אֲבֹתָיו

13   פֶּן־תִּדְרֹשׁ לֵאלֹהֵיהֶם

Lessons 41–42
Words 1–260

1   וְזֹאת הַמִּצְוָה הַחֻקִּים וְהַמִּשְׁפָּטִים אֲשֶׁר צִוָּה יְהוָה אֱלֹהֵיכֶם

2   כָּל־הַנְּחָלִים הֹלְכִים אֶל־הַיָּם

3   לִקְבֹּר אֶת־מֵתִי מִלְּפָנָי

4   לְמַעַן חַלֵּל אֶת־שֵׁם קָדְשִׁי

5   וְהֵבִיא אֶת־הַפָּר לִפְנֵי יְהוָה

6   נִכְרֹת עֲצֵי לְבָנוֹן

7   וַיַּאֲמִינוּ בַּיהוָה וּבְמֹשֶׁה עַבְדּוֹ

8   וָאֲקַבְּצָה מִיִּשְׂרָאֵל רָאשִׁים לַעֲלוֹת עִמִּי

9   וְלֹא־נַשְׁאַר בָּהֶם אִישׁ

10   הֵחֵל לִדְרוֹשׁ לֵאלֹהֵי דָוִיד

11   מִשְׁפְּטֵי־יְהוָה אֱמֶת צָדְקוּ יַחְדָּו

12   וְעַתָּה יִגְדַּל־נָא כֹּחַ אֲדֹנָי

13   וְהַכֹּהֲנִים הַנֹּשְׂאֵי הָאָרוֹן הַבְּרִית

14   וְהִשְׁאִיר אַחֲרָיו בְּרָכָה

15   פֶּן־תִּכְרֹת בְּרִית לְיוֹשֵׁב הָאָרֶץ

16   וּמַרְאֶה הָעֶרֶב וְהַבֹּקֶר

VOCABULARY

Lessons 43–44

Words 1–270

1 אַל־תַּשְׁלִיכֵנִי מִלְּפָנֶיךָ וְרוּחַ קָדְשְׁךָ אַל־תִּקַּח מִמֶּנִּי

2 כָּל־קְהַל יִשְׂרָאֵל

3 וַיְהִי אוֹר

4 וַיַּגֵּשׁ אֵת פַּר הַחַטָּאת

5 וַאֲנַחְנוּ חֲשַׁבְנֻהוּ נָגוּעַ מֻכֵּה אֱלֹהִים וּמְעֻנֶּה

6 עֶצֶם מֵעֲצָמַי וּבָשָׂר מִבְּשָׂרִי

7 וְנִשְׁתַּחֲוֶה וְנָשׁוּבָה אֲלֵיכֶם

8 זֶרַע עָוֹן לֹא יִירַשׁ אֵת נַחֲלָתִי

9 מִיּוֹם לְיוֹם וּמֵחֹדֶשׁ לְחֹדֶשׁ

10 מְעַט וְרָעִים הָיוּ יְמֵי שְׁנֵי חַיַּי

Lessons 45–46

Words 1–280

1 וְיֹאכְלוּ מִפְּרִי דַרְכָּם

2 וְיָשַׁבְתָּ עִמּוֹ יָמִים אֲחָדִים עַד אֲשֶׁר־תָּשׁוּב חֲמַת אָחִיךָ

3 וּלְשׁוֹנוּ כְּאֵשׁ אֹכָלֶת

4 וַיַּרְא וְהִנֵּה הָהָר מָלֵא סוּסִים וְרֶכֶב אֵשׁ סְבִיבֹת אֱלִישָׁע

5 הִנֵּה כְתוּבָה עַל־סֵפֶר הַיָּשָׁר

6 בְּטַח בַּיהוה וַעֲשֵׂה־טוֹב

7 הִנֵּה אֲדֹנָי מַעֲלֶה עֲלֵיהֶם אֶת־מֵי הַנָּהָר הָעֲצוּמִים וְהָרַבִּים אֶת־מֶלֶךְ אַשּׁוּר וְאֶת־כָּל־כְּבוֹדוֹ

134

8   אָמְרוּ נִלְכְּדָה בָבֶל

9   כִּי־עַתָּה שַׁבְנוּ זֶה פַעֲמָיִם

10   בָּאֵשׁ יִשְׂרְפוּ אֹתוֹ וְאֶתְהֶן

Lessons 47–48

Words 1–290

1   עַל נַהֲרוֹת בָּבֶל שָׁם יָשַׁבְנוּ גַּם־בָּכִינוּ בְּזָכְרֵנוּ אֶת־צִיּוֹן

2   הוֹדוּ לַיהוה כִּי־טוֹב כִּי לְעוֹלָם חַסְדּוֹ

3   צֶדֶק לָבַשְׁתִּי וַיִּלְבָּשֵׁנִי

4   לֹא תֵאָכֵל בָּאֵשׁ תִּשָּׂרֵף

5   הָיוּ בְנֵי־יִשְׂרָאֵל מְקַטְּרִים לוֹ

6   רַק הַדָּם לֹא תֹאכֵלוּ עַל־הָאָרֶץ תִּשְׁפְּכֶנּוּ כַּמָּיִם

7   זָכוֹר אֶת־יוֹם הַשַּׁבָּת לְקַדְּשׁוֹ

8   וַיָּשֶׂם יהוה לְקַיִן אוֹת (a sign) לְבִלְתִּי הַכּוֹת־אֹתוֹ כָּל־מֹצְאוֹ

9   שִׁבְעַת יָמִים תְּכַפֵּר עַל־הַמִּזְבֵּחַ וְקִדַּשְׁתָּ אֹתוֹ

10   הֲתִשְׁפֹּט אֹתָם הֲתִשְׁפּוֹט בֶּן־אָדָם אֶת־תּוֹעֲבֹת אֲבוֹתָם הוֹדִיעֵם׃

11   כְּגִבּוֹרִים יְרֻצוּן יַעֲלוּ חוֹמָה

12   דִּבֶּר שְׁקָרִים הוּא

13   מִפְּנֵי אֲשֶׁר קִטְּרָתֶם וַאֲשֶׁר חֲטָאתֶם לַיהוה וְלֹא שְׁמַעְתֶּם בְּקוֹל יהוה
וּבְתֹרָתוֹ וּבְחֻקֹּתָיו וּבְעֵדְוֹתָיו לֹא הֲלַכְתֶּם עַל־כֵּן קָרָאת אֶתְכֶם הָרָעָה
הַזֹּאת כַּיּוֹם הַזֶּה׃

VOCABULARY

Lessons 49–50

Words 1–300

1 נַחֲמוּ נַחֲמוּ עַמִּי יֹאמַר אֱלֹהֵיכֶם

2 בְּךָ בָטְחוּ וְלֹא־בוֹשׁוּ

3 וַיְהִי מִסְפַּר הָעֹלָה אֲשֶׁר הֵבִיאוּ הַקָּהָל בָּקָר שִׁבְעִים אֵילִים מֵאָה כְּבָשִׂים מָאתַיִם לְעֹלָה לַיהוה כָּל־אֵלֶּה:

4 וְאַרְבָּעָה פָנִים לְאֶחָת וְאַרְבַּע כְּנָפַיִם לְאַחַת לָהֶם

5 שֵׁשׁ שֶׁבַע שְׁמֹנֶה

6 אֶל־גְּבוּל אֱדוֹם בַּנֶּגְבָּה

7 כִּי־אַתָּה עַם־עָנִי תּוֹשִׁיעַ

8 הֲרִימוֹת יְמִין צָרָיו הִשְׂמַחְתָּ כָּל־אוֹיְבָיו:

9 לַעֲשׂוֹת בַּזָּהָב וּבַכֶּסֶף וּבַנְּחֹשֶׁת

10 כָּל־הַבְּכוֹר אֲשֶׁר יִוָּלֵד בִּבְקָרְךָ וּבְצֹאנְךָ הַזָּכָר תַּקְדִּישׁ לַיהוה אֱלֹהֶיךָ וְהָיִיתָ אַךְ שָׂמֵחַ:

Lessons 51–52

Words 1–310

1 וַיְהִי רָעָב בָּאָרֶץ וַיֵּרֶד אַבְרָם מִצְרַיְמָה

2 לְכוּ דִרְשׁוּ אֶת־יהוה בַּעֲדִי

3 וַיְהִי בַּחֲצִי הַלַּיְלָה וַיהוה הִכָּה כָל־בְּכוֹר בְּאֶרֶץ מִצְרַיִם

4 וַיֹּאמֶר הַגֹּאֵל לֹא־אוּכַל לִגְאָל־לִי

5 וְאַמָּה וָחֵצִי רָחְבָּהּ

6 כָּל־הַנֹּגֵעַ בָּהֶם יִטְמָא

7   שׁוּב לְאַרְצְךָ וְאֵישִׁיבָה עִמָּךְ

8   וְחַטָּאתִי נֶגְדִּי תָמִיד

9   אִם־אֶשְׁכָּחֵךְ יְרוּשָׁלָ͏ִם תִּשְׁכַּח יְמִינִי

10   רַק הָעָם מְזַבְּחִים בַּבָּמוֹת

11   אַף־אֲנִי אֶעֱשֶׂה־זֹּאת לָכֶם

12   לָכֵן נְאֻם יהוה אֱלֹהֵי יִשְׂרָאֵל

13   וְאֶת־אוֹיְבֵיהֶם כִּסָּה הַיָּם

ANSWERS

Lesson 1

Particles and words 1–10

a son	7			and	1
he went up	8			for, because, surely	2
in, by (as in by means of)	9			he was, it was/happened	3
to, for	10			which, who, because	4
a sacrifice	11			to	5
no, not (negates what follows)	12			a daughter	6

Lesson 2

Words 1–20

he entered/came	8			a deed	1
his day	9			and Lot said	2
he turned	10			the whole, all	3
his house	11			to a land	4
in it, in him, by him	12			Adonai made	5
his sons	13			his son	6
to enter	14			kingdom	7

Lesson 3

Words 1–30

to his people	6			and Joseph heard/listened	1
Isaac made, did	7			from a wilderness	2
God gave to him	8			in/by his hand	3

she, that one (f.)   9

his face   10

he saw a sight/vision   4

and Saul went   5

Lesson 4

Words 1–40

he did not take   7

(the place) on top   8

one house   9

these (m. or f.)   10

to return   11

this is he   12

behold, a daughter!   1

and the father dwelled/sat with him   2

as far as Moab   3

and Isaac went out   4

the man returned to his city   5

the man ruled because he was king   6

Lesson 5

Words 1–50

on him/it   8

his death   9

this (f.)   10

year   11

who did not serve   12

he returned/turned back   13

he is dead/he died   14

I am not Mordeḥai   1

and he sent   2

in the hand of Adonai   3

and he heard and he knew   4

the servant of Elijah   5

face to face   6

his name (is/was) Samson   7

Lesson 6

Words 1–60

the eyes of all Israel are on him	1
and they died	2
he ate	3
what and why	4
two	5
you are the man and moreover, a priest	6
and all the kings knew	7
and they came, the servants of Absalom (and the servants of Absalom came), to the woman	8
behold the father who did not say a word to his son	9
with עִם if אִם name שֵׁם there שָׁם	10

Lesson 7

Words 1–70

you (m.pl.)	1
the ways of Zion	2
his person, self, life	3
the others	4
and he returned to the place and he called there (in) the name of Adonai	5
I am the first	6
like a sister	7
behind, after	8
therefore	9
he got up	10
he saw the evil	11
and Abraham lifted his eyes	12
there are no priests in the House of Adonai	13

Lesson 8

Words 1–80

thus said Adonai	1
one hundred	2
Adam/humankind is from the earth	3
all the nations of the earth/land	4
and David put the words/matters in his heart	5
and he got up and he went to the top of the mountain	6
surely this is my master/lord	7

Lesson 9

Words 1–90

there is no water	1
a voice is calling	2
the pillars of the house	3
under him/it	4
he lived	5
the servants did not sit because you (m. pl.) were standing	6
and he will go out and pass by/cross over to the mountain	7
a thousand one hundred	8
my head	9
and he grew up/became great	10
twenty	11
he bore	12
Is Joseph still alive?	13

VOCABULARY

―――

Lesson 10

Words 1–100

holy am I therefore you are holy	1
and they will serve Adonai forever	2
Adonai commanded David, who was going (walking) with the army	3
and the guard called to the poor man (who was) sitting in the house of Adonai	4
now is the time	5
on account of the commandment	6
Adonai will guard my way	7
and they found Saul there	8
Who is the man who did not cross the Jordan?	9
the mouth of the king	10

Lessons 11–12

Words 1–110

and it was thus	1
and he answered and said	2
she among all the princes of Israel	3
the big chief	4
three priests	5
and they went—Pharaoh and all Egypt—into the midst of the sea	6
Adonai made the heaven and the earth	7
And Goliath took his sword in his hand and said, "Who is the man who has a lot of silver?" And no one said a word.	8
Who are you, my son?	9
and the judge judged the people of Israel	10
a time to bear (or: be born) and a time to die	11
the man feared my lord, the king	12

ANSWERS

Lessons 13–14

Words 1–120

and I came down	1
we became great/grew up	2
to see	3
to go down	4
you/they (f. pl.) will send	5
we will serve	6
under the wood	7
his two youths	8
the fire of Adonai fell from heaven	9
Adonai will reign forever	10
and a wind/spirit lifted Ezekiel and he came to Jerusalem	11
And the daughter of the king grew up and her father gave to her an ox, and she said, "What is this you are giving me?"	12
and they sacrificed sacrifices on the altar (place of sacrifice)	13
and they went, the two of them, together	14
he lived and he died	15

Lessons 15–16

Words 1–130

you/they (f. pl.) will serve	9		there is no blood on my hands	1
you ate	10		five angels/messengers	2
the third day	11		she sat in her tent	3
I blessed	12		these are the heads of the nations	4
living water(s)	13		one ram	5
and she/you (m. sg.) put	14		a good year	6
his seed	15		the gate of heaven	7
Who loves a wicked woman?	16		and he built there an altar	8

VOCABULARY

Lessons 17–18

Words 1–140

and you will give to me bread	1
seven rams (are) coming	2
great is the war	3
forty stones	4
the sun (it) is in heaven	5
and he will die—the man who did lie with her	6
you (f. pl.) feared	7
the angel touched him	8
we abandoned	9
the stone, which Jacob put, was like a pillar	10

Lessons 19–20

Words 1–150

northward and southward	1
you (m. pl.) will go forth to battle against your enemies	2
Adonai made the sea	3
my enemy will not return to his father	4
from this evil family/clan	5
like the dust of the earth	6
and you/they (f.) drew near to the face of (presence of) Elazar the priest	7
in my midst	8
garments of holiness are they (they are holy garments)	9
and he turned westward /seaward	10
and Esther was clothed in royalty	11

144

Lessons 21–22

Words 1–160

not so (thus) the wicked	1
Rachel gathered the sheep, which were her father's	2
take your staff and stretch your hand over the water(s) of Egypt	3
hand in place of hand, and foot in place of foot	4
and they came after (behind) them—Pharaoh and all his army—into the midst of the sea	5
the sea is full of water	6
you (m. sg.)/ she will sleep on your bed this night	7
and they will take other stones	8
give (f. sg.) to me bread and meat	9
surely your loving kindness is great unto heaven	10

Lessons 23–24

Words 1–170

he was able	1
write (m. pl.) to your mother and to your father	2
seek and you will find	3
. . . and his heart died within him and he became a stone	4
Eve, she (is) mother of all living (things)	5
the youth remembered	6
loving kindness, well-being, and strength	7
we heard that the enemies had become great and their sons took possession of our borders	8
and behold Rachel coming with the sheep, which were her father's	9
do not (m.pl.) approach a woman	10

Lessons 25–26

Words 1–180

they gave voice in the house of Adonai as on a day of assembly/festival	1
a time to drink or a time to eat	2
she abandoned	3
the leader turned and went out	4
and it was morning	5
four, five, six	6
your Torot (teachings)	7
my messenger/angel	8
he will love	9
the congregation of Israel	10
you (f. sg.) served and did not perish	11
the king will write for himself a Torah	12

Lessons 27–28

Words 1–190

swear שׁבע	*prepare* כון	*deliver* נצל	*save* ישׁע	1
cubit אַמָּה	*mother* אֵם	*what* מָה	*hundred* מֵאָה	2

the camp of the Levites	3
take (m. sg.) Aaron and his sons . . . and the garments	4
and I will gather them to the midst of the city	5
A righteous man, who will find?	6
and he put the vessels in his tent	7
in order to know the generations of the sons of Israel	8
and the king, David, was old	9
and she came to him and he lay with her	10
visit, pray	11
a sin he sinned	12

to increase (add to) 13

and the wicked one, surely he will turn from all his sins which he did 14

we will encamp 15

and God finished his work which he had made 16

Lessons 29–30

Words 1–200

the evil was finished 1

and my glory to another I will not give 2

good oils 3

they hated him—the brothers of Joseph 4

and now he will raise my head over my enemies 5

and I put my life in my hands 6

Are your brothers not shepherding in Shechem? 7

God has given us eyes for seeing, ears for hearing, and feet/legs for walking 8

and I will uncover your heart 9

Elijah the prophet 10

and the battle (war) was heavy on (against) Saul 11

and he took three staffs in his hand 12

Lessons 31–32

Words 1–210

and they will inherit the field of Ephraim 1

the remainder 2

he chose us to be a holy people to him (his holy people) 3

and Israel camped there in front of the mountain 4

go and (you will) gather the elders of Israel 5

and Eli perceived /understood that Adonai was calling the boy 6 on the edge (lip) of the sea 7

ask (m. pl.) for the peace of Jerusalem 8

a generation goes and a generation comes, but the earth stands forever 9

great (big) is the place between them 10

write this in a document/letter 11

take the animal of the Levites instead of their animal 12

according to the number of the tribes of Israel 13

Lessons 33–34

Words 1–220

from outside the camp 1

to understand between good and evil 2

and I will kill you (m. pl.) with a sword 3

and he was sitting at the opening of the tent 4

she'll be comin' 'round the mountain 5

and you (f. sg.) will not call me any longer "my husband" 6

and we will flee before them, and they will journey to my lord 7

do not (m. sg.) spill blood 8

and their sin, surely it is very heavy 9

surely you have not abandoned those seeking you, Adonai 10

and if not, tell (m. pl.) me 11

Lessons 35–36

Words 1–230

a mighty man of strength and a man of war 1

who is like you, Adonai 2

ask your father and he will tell you 3

148

and the young girl was good in his eyes   4

and you will do according to your wisdom   5

Who put a mouth to Adam? i.e., Who has given humankind speech?   6

surely evil I am bringing from the north   7

let the heaven(s) rejoice (the heavens will rejoice)   8

and this is the teaching (law) of the minḥa (offering)   9

these are the statutes which Adonai is commanding you today   10

and the Israelites encamped opposite them   11

and Moses raised his hand and smote the rock   12

I alone am seeking Adonai in order to bring (near) burnt offerings of 200 rams   13

my lord will speak because you have strengthened me   14

Lessons 37–38

Words 1–240

he journeyed but did not flee!   1

and they added still to hating him (and they hated him even more)   2

wine I did not drink   3

break (f. sg.) a leg   4

Have I not caused you to hear since then?   5

praise the name of Adonai; praise, servants of Adonai   6

(those) who are standing in the house of Adonai; in the courts of the house of our God   7

I will not destroy if I will find there forty and five   8

surely the hand of Adonai will rest upon this mountain   9

because/surely God has come out before you to smite the camp of the Philistines   10

and you did not trust (have faith) in him   11

surely we are consumed in your anger   12

to go before me in truth   13

Why have you forgotten me?   14

VOCABULARY

Lessons 39–40

Words 1–250

open for me the gates of righteousness 1

the right hand of Adonai makes strength (does valiantly) 2

you (m. sg.) will build the walls of Jerusalem 3

go down (m. pl.) to meet Midian 4

how good are your tents, Jacob, your dwelling places, Israel 5

and it will be when he sits on the throne of his kingdom 6

and the glory of Adonai dwelled on Mount Sinai 7

justice, justice you will pursue 8

Is Adonai in our midst or not? 9

concerning all his/its vessels you will make (them) of bronze 10

and Jehosephat said to the king of Israel as I am so you are, as my people so your people, as my 11
horses so your horses

a man in the inheritance of the tribe of his fathers 12

lest you will seek their gods 13

Lessons 41–42

Words 1–260

and this is the commandment, the statutes and the judgments, which Adonai your God 1
commanded you

all wadis (rivers) go to the sea 2

to bury my dead away from my face/presence 3

in order to profane my holy name 4

and he will bring the bull before Adonai 5

we will cut the tress of Lebanon 6

and they had faith in Adonai and in Moses his servant 7

and I gathered chiefs from Israel to go up with me 8

and we will not leave a man among them 9

he began to seek the God of David   10

the judgments of Adonai are truth; they are righteous altogether   11

and now let the strength of my Lord be great   12

and the priests who were lifting the ark of the covenant   13

he will leave a blessing after him   14

lest you cut a covenant with the inhabitant of the land   15

and the sight (vision) of the evening and the morning   16

Lessons 43–44

Words 1–270

do not cast me from before you; and your holy spirit do not take from me   1

all the congregation of Israel   2

and there was light   3

and he brought near the bull of/for the sin offering   4

and we, we considered him stricken, smitten by God and afflicted   5

bone of my bones and flesh of my flesh   6

and we will prostrate ourselves in worship and we will return to you   7

a seed of wickedness will not take possession of my inheritance   8

from day to day and from month to month   9

few and bad have been the days of the years of my life   10

Lessons 45–46

Words 1–280

and they will eat of the fruit of their way   1

and you will stay with him a few days until your brother's fury returns (turns away)   2

and his tongue [is/was] like a consuming fire   3

and he looked and behold the mountain was full of horses and chariotry of fire around Elisha   4

behold, it is written on/in the document of the upright   5

trust in Adonai and do good   6

behold, the Lord is bringing up on them the water of the river mighty and many, the king of   7
Assyria and all his glory

say (m. pl.) "Babylon is captured"   8

surely now we have returned this two times   9

with fire they will burn him and them (f. pl.)   10

Lessons 47–48

Words 1–290

by the rivers of Babylon there we sat, aye, we wept when we remembered   1
(in our remembering) Zion

Give thanks to Adonai, surely (because) he is good, surely his loving kindness is forever   2

righteousness I wore and it clothed me   3

it will not be eaten; with fire it will be burned   4

the sons of Israel were burning incense to him   5

only the blood you will not eat; you will pour it on the ground like water   6

remember the Sabbath day to sanctify it   7

and Adonai put on Cain a sign that anyone who finds him not smite him   8

seven days you will make atonement for the altar and sanctify it   9

Will you judge them, will you judge, son of man? The abomination of their fathers cause them   10
to know

Like (strong) men they run, they go up a wall   11

A speaker of falsehoods is he   12

Because you burned incense and sinned against Adonai and did not listen to the voice of Adonai   13
and in his Torot (teachings) and his statutes and his testimonies you did not walk, therefore this
evil has befallen you as on this day.

Lessons 49–50

Words 1–300

comfort, comfort my people says your God 1

in you they trusted and were not ashamed 2

and the number of burnt offering(s), which the congregation brought, (was) seventy 3

oxen, a hundred rams, two hundred sheep, all these for a burnt offering to Adonai 4
and four faces to each one and four pairs of wings to each one of them

six, seven, eight 5

to the border of Edom, to the southland 6

surely, you, an afflicted people you will save 7

you raised the right hand of his adversaries; you caused all of his enemies to rejoice 8

to make with gold and silver and bronze 9

Every first-born male that is born among the cattle and among the sheep you will sanctify to the 10
Lord your God, and you will be, ach, (surely) happy!

Lessons 51–52

Words 1–310

and there was a famine in the land and Avram went down to Egypt 1

go seek (m. pl.) Adonai on my behalf 2

and it was at midnight that Adonai smote all the firstborn in the land of Egypt 3

and the redeemer said, "I am not able to redeem for myself" 4

and its (f. referent) width: a cubit and a half 5

everyone (all) who touches them will be impure 6

return to your land and I will deal well with you 7

and my sin is before me daily 8

if I forget you, Jerusalem, let my right hand forget 9

only the people were sacrificing in the high places 10

I, for my part (indeed), will do this for you (m. pl.) 11

therefore the word of Adonai, God of Israel 12

(and) the sea covered their enemies 13